CASTLE RUINS OF MEDIEVAL ENGLAND AND WALES

GÜNTER ENDRES AND
GRAHAM HOBSTER

D1565820

Airlife

Copyright © The Crowood Press Ltd 2003

Text written by Günter Endres
Photography by Graham Hobster
Maps created by Peter Harper

First published in the UK in 2003 by
Airlife Publishing, an imprint of The Crowood Press Ltd

British Library Cataloguing-in-Publication Data
  A catalogue record for this book
  is available from the British Library.

ISBN 1 84037 419 5

Printed in Hong Kong

Airlife Publishing
An imprint of The Crowood Press Ltd
Ramsbury, Marlborough
Wiltshire, SN8 2HR

www.crowood.com

Contents

Foreword

Many lofty hills throughout the English and Welsh landscapes are crowned with broken stone castles from a bygone age. Some are mere fragments of rubble walls, others still dominate their surroundings in a defiant gesture. All still draw passer-by and visitor alike. How can one explain this determination to climb precipitous crags and explore the vestiges of great keeps and once splendid but now empty halls? Is it a sense of history, or merely a fascination with our occasionally chivalrous, but more often bloody, past? Could it be admiration for the achievements of the master military architects, or do we stand in awe of the absolute power over life and death once held by kings and noblemen? Are we pacing the ruined battlements fully armed and unflinching to repel imagined raiders? For everyone, this experience is different. As we climb the soaring towers and survey the splendid views from our lofty position, we are reminded that many of these crumbling fortresses were built nearly a thousand years ago. How they have survived over the centuries against constant military onslaught, intrigue and final slighting, followed by neglect and the destructive effects of the elements, is quite miraculous. It is also a celebration of continuity in the face of adversity.

We have visited all the castle remains described in this book and have taken numerous photographs, both in glorious sunshine and in conditions less kind to the lens. Our selection, while limited by the restrictions of size, has been made to illustrate the most imposing towers and gatehouses on each site, as well as some of the fascinating military architectural and engineering details that have survived in many defensive strongholds and fortified mansions. It is hoped that these might encourage a visit when in the vicinity, or travelling from afar. The text to accompany the photographs, while still requiring a great deal of research, is to a large extent a compilation, drawing on other people's writings, especially to summarise the always interesting histories of the various castles. We owe a great debt of gratitude to all.

It is unrealistic to expect to be able to include all the numerous castles that have survived in some ruined form in England and Wales, however laudable such an attempt would be. But we believe that there are no major omissions in our coverage, which also includes a few that, in spite of very scant remains, can be justified for their historical significance, or because they are shrouded in mystery, legend and intrigue. Please enjoy this tour through medieval England and Wales – we most certainly did.

Günter Endres and Graham Hobster

Castle building in England and Wales

It is surprising to learn that there were no Anglo-Saxon castles prior to the Norman Conquest. Some historians have suggested that a few private fortifications may have existed under Edward the Confessor immediately before, but this has not been proven. The relatively united governance of England and the absence of a feudal system as practised in continental Europe rendered the requirement for military strongholds to control populations and land largely unnecessary. This all changed, however, when William of Normandy landed at Pevensey in 1066 and immediately began erecting a fortified enclosure inside the old Roman fort on the Saxon Shore, before defeating King Harold II at the Battle of Hastings, and changing the course of history. William is said to have brought with him prefabricated timber sections which enabled him to erect the enclosure in a single day! Before the end of the year, the Conqueror had been crowned King of England as William I, and so began a period of castle building that was to last nearly 600 years.

William I built the great rectangular tower at Colchester

The Normans were expert in the speedy construction of castles to control and defend their territorial gains, using large gangs of forced labour. These early fortifications, many built within a fortnight, consisted of mounds of earth raised from a circular ditch, whose flat top was surmounted by a wooden tower (donjon) in the middle and ringed by a wooden palisade. The tower was the focal point of the castle, used as a watchtower and residence for the lord, and would normally also have included offices, a kitchen and a chapel. It also served as the last line of defence should the larger outer defensive area (bailey), again enclosed by timber palisades, fall to the enemy. The bailey either surrounded the mound or was built alongside it, being accessed by a wooden bridge across the ditch. A second bailey was added to a number of castles where extra security was required. In some instances, natural hills or rocky outcrops were adapted to facilitate construction, but where an artificial mound was thrown up, the loose soil was reinforced with rock to

Most early fortifications were erected on a natural or artificial motte, with the timber towers later replaced by shell keeps as here at Launceston

prevent it collapsing. The V-shaped ditches also often had stone or timber revetments to hold the earth together. Ditches were generally dry, but where it was possible to divert rivers or streams to create a wet ditch, or moat, this was considered preferable and added to the defensive strength of the castle.

Known as motte or motte-and-bailey castles, these tall structures, reaching in some instances to a height of over 30m (100ft), dwarfed their surroundings and were designed to strike terror into the hearts of the local population and keep them subjugated. More than 200 such castles were raised during the reigns of the Conqueror and his third son William II (Rufus), with many more following in the first half of the twelth century. William I was himself responsible for building several of these early castles, but the majority were erected by his knights on land granted as reward for their loyal support during the invasion and subsequent victory. Almost every castle was strategically sited to command key roads, towns, river crossings, harbours and coastal stretches, or was built on high ground to dominate extensive land holdings.

Cast in Stone

Of these first timber castles nothing has survived, although numerous mottes can still be seen dotting the countryside. The timber fortifications were susceptible to fire and decay and were probably always intended as an interim measure to establish control in the quickest time possible. But to reinforce their ruthless subjugation of England and Wales, the Normans recognised that more permanent structures were required. In part, this determination was expressed by replacing the original timber palisades with stone curtain walls and the wooden tower with a more durable circular shell-keep, but the most impressive early stone structures were the massive rectangular great towers built by William I, particularly those at London and Colchester. The towers were typically three or four storeys high, with mural chambers opening off the single main rooms on each floor. Straight or spiral stairs, often built into the thickness of the wall, connected all main floors, also giving access to the basement which was used for storage. Much of the stone for early Norman castles came from the quarries at Caen, which produced a fine creamy limestone, but later construction used stone from local quarries, particularly from Barnack in Northamptonshire. Smooth ashlar blocks were often used as facings.

Such menacing structures, characterised by their sheer size, exceptionally thick walls and projecting buttresses, were highly effective against a frontal attack, with single entry generally through a strong doorway at first-floor level, accessed by a flight of stairs. Extra protection was later provided by a forebuilding, which more often than not also housed a chapel on the upper level. If attackers did manage to penetrate the outer defences, they were faced by a strong cross-wall that divided most great towers. In addition to providing a further obstacle to besiegers, the cross-walls, usually placed centrally or slightly off-centre, also served as structural strengthening for the tower. Window openings at the lower levels were small on the outside, but were splayed on the inside to let in more light. The relatively flimsy timber or tiled roofs in early castles were most vulnerable to attack by missiles or flaming arrows, but this problem was overcome by carrying the outer walls up beyond roof level and creating battlemented fighting platforms. The base of the tower was covered by wooden platforms, known as hoardings, suspended from the wall. Curtain walls were subsequently built with projecting towers, which obviated the need for wooden hoardings.

Gundulf, Bishop of Rochester, was one of the early military architects responsible for building the great tower-keep at Rochester Castle

The Norman castle-building programme was continued relentlessly by William II and taken a step further under the long reign of Henry I, when stone had almost totally replaced timber as the material of choice. Robert de Bellême and Archbishop Lanfranc's master builder Gundulf, Bishop of Rochester, were the most important architects of the time. Many of the surviving castles of the period were built in an orderly progression under royal direction, but this was thrown into turmoil during the Anarchy of Stephen of Blois and Matilda when more than 1,100 adulterine (unlicensed) castles were built throughout the realm by barons and minor nobility. The *Anglo-Saxon Chronicle* recorded: 'And they filled the whole land with these castles. They sorely burdened the unhappy people of the country with forced labour on the castles. And when the castles were made they filled them with devils and wicked men.' Most had very short lives, for when Matilda's son Henry II came to the throne in 1154, he set about confiscating and destroying the great majority of these private enterprises before himself embarking on a large programme of royal castle-building, which was carried through with equal vigour by his sons, Richard I and John.

All the while, refinements were added to enhance the military effectiveness of the royal fortresses and those licensed to loyal supporters, including portcullised tower gatehouses with murder holes in the ceiling of the entrance porch from which rocks, hot iron and other materials could be dropped on those foolhardy enough to try and gain access. Battlemented wall-walks with the various sections linked by movable bridges, permitted each to be isolated if one part fell to an attacker. But the most significant change was the gradual move away from the rectangular keep towards circular or polygonal towers, which were less susceptible to mining since they had no vulnerable corners, and to the great siege engines of the day. Among the first proponents of the new shape was Henry's leading expert, Maurice the Engineer, but already the reliance on the keep as the major defensive stronghold was declining, especially once a circuit of outer ramparts had begun to take the first brunt of any assault.

Castles by their very nature had been austere places where defensive requirements took precedence, but a distinct tendency towards more comfortable living was creeping in, often brushing aside military considerations. The upper living quarters of the lord or appointed castellan were provided with large windows, later glazed, ornate fireplaces and garderobes, while richly decorated chapels took care of the spiritual side. During the minority of Henry III his guardian, Hubert de Burgh, spent considerable sums on improving the royal castles in this way. Once of age, Henry threw himself enthusiastically into maintaining and enhancing his castles and is particularly remembered for creating the vast lake-fortress of Kenilworth out of an ordinary defensive structure that did not have the advantage of being sited on a high and impregnable rock. Henry considered water as the most effective means of keeping siege engines far enough away from the curtain walls to nullify their great threat.

The massive, twin-towered gatehouse eventually replaced the keep as the main defensive structure

Surrounding a castle with water was seen during Henry III's time as the best means to keep siege-engines away from the curtain walls

The Edwardian Castles

The borderland between England and Wales has always been an area of contention, going back at least as far as the Iron Age. In the first centuries A.D. the Romans established forts to control the rebellious Welsh, and the Anglo-Saxon king Offa of Mercia built the famous Offa's Dyke in the eighth century as a physical barrier between the two lands. These efforts, however, did little to stop the border conflicts, but when the Saxon *thegn* Eadric the Wild and his Welsh allies rebelled against the Norman conquerors, William I created three powerful earldoms along the marches, at Chester, Shrewsbury and Hereford, to protect his kingdom. The word 'march' comes from the Anglo-Saxon *meare*, meaning boundary or frontier area, and the area collectively became known as the Welsh Marches. In addition to the three marcher lordships, which controlled a vast swathe of borderlands, William I and William II also established many smaller earldoms as reward for their most valued supporters. The earls were given extensive judicial powers and ruled their lands much as they liked, raising their own castles and militia without the need for royal consent, in part financing such extravagance with taxes importuned from the local population. The defence of the realm and extension of Norman influence into much of Wales was all the king demanded in return. The marcher lords built numerous motte-and-bailey castles along the border and also established boroughs or towns as administrative and economic centres.

Subduing the Welsh was quite another matter, in spite of this show of force. From time to time, various Welsh princes tried to throw off the Norman yoke, raiding and sacking the poorly defended castles. But these were sporadic attempts until Llywelyn the Last, who had united the disparate factions as Prince of Wales, finally spurred Edward I into decisive action after he refused to pay homage to him. Edward's three campaigns against the Welsh in 1277, 1282–3 and 1294–5 ushered in a short, but great, era of castle building, the results of which deservedly became known as the 'Edwardian castles'. Distinguished by its concentric layout, of which Caerphilly, started a few years before by the Red Earl of Gloucester, was the precursor, the new design incorporated all the latest defensive technologies. It comprised a double set of rectangular or polygonal curtains pierced by massive symmetrically placed towers, and an immensely strong gatehouse, which was itself a powerful fortress that guarded the castle's most vulnerable side.

Beaumaris was the last of the great Edwardian Castles to be built in Wales. The favoured design then was concentric, essentially a castle within a castle

Native Welsh castles were noted for their lofty positions dominated by massive circular or apsidal tower keeps, as here at Dolbadarn

The Edwardian programme, aimed at imposing his control over all of Wales once and for all, was enormously ambitious and expensive. It included the remodelling of four royal border castles, four new 'lordship' castles, the remodelling and rebuilding of three native Welsh castles, and the construction of ten new royal castles. Between 1277 and 1304, a total of £80,000 was spent, with another £15,000 up to 1330. Nearly 10,000 workmen had to be recruited from all over England and Wales. The vast project was carried through with the help of one of the greatest architects of the Middle Ages, James of St George, assisted by Walter of Hereford. James came from Savoy, with which Edward had a family connection, and served for over thirty years, adopting the concentric design whenever possible. He was soon given the title of Master of the King's Works in Wales, and for three years, from 1290 to 1293 was Constable of Harlech,

one of the spectacular castles he designed and built. The Edwardian castles in Wales were interspersed with native fortresses, many built on virtually inaccessible rocky outcrops and very much based on Norman principles, although the two-storey apsidal tower can be described as a typically Welsh design. After Edward's subjugation of Wales, most were left to decay, until Owain Glyndwr tried unsuccessfully to regain Wales from the English in the early fifteenth Century, when some were repaired and refortified.

On the northern border, frequent raids by the Scots in the thirteenth and fourteenth centuries also saw the building of many formidable castles. However, the great era of the military fortress was almost over. The decline of the castle was due to a combination of factors, including the discovery of gunpowder and much later, the use of heavy cannon, which many castles were unable to withstand, although those that were taken fell to a combination of bombardment and starvation. There was also an increasing tendency to fight large battles on open ground, and a change in the social fabric of medieval England. Noblemen loyal to the Crown were allowed to fortify their splendid manor houses in increasing numbers, adding a semblance of strength, more for show and status than for true defensive purposes. The first such licence 'to fortify and crenellate a wall of stone and lime' had been issued by Richard I in 1195, and this trend, while at first slow to take hold, became prevalent in the fourteenth and fifteenth centuries. When Antiquarian John Leland toured the country in 1540–42, he reported that castles everywhere were 'nearly down', or 'far gone to decay.'

The Last Throw

The last throw of the dice came in the sixteenth century under Henry VIII, whose system of coastal defences marked the last great epoch of castle building. Henry's castles were generally of circular or cloverleaf design, squat in appearance and well defended, with inner and outer areas separated by a well-commanded ditch. They stretched along the south coast and were sited to defend the king's new fleet of ships.

The final chapter in the 600-year span of castle building in medieval England was written during the Civil War which tore the country apart in the years 1642–49. All royal strongholds were besieged and eventually taken. After the end of the war, those that had not been brought down by bombardment were ordered by Parliament to be deliberately slighted (destroyed). Stone was subsequently pillaged for other buildings and neglect and weather contributed to the dilapidation. The preservation efforts of the Ministry of Works in the early twentieth century, continued under English Heritage, CADW Welsh Historic Monuments and the National Trust, helped to preserve many of these evocative ruins, and with them much of our history. The beauty of castles is that no two are alike, their design having been governed by topographical considerations, money, materials and the personal preference of the king or lord. Each is unique and, in its own way, spectacular.

Contacts: English Heritage
www.english-heritage.org.uk
National Trust
www.nationaltrust.org.uk
CADW
www.cadw-wales.gov.uk

For further reading

Brian Bailey: *The Ordnance Survey Book of Great British Ruins*; Cassell, London, 1991.

Bal J Ivo: *Strongholds of the Barons*; Arnold Fairbairns, London, 1906.

Richard Humble: *English Castles*; Weidenfeld and Nicolson, London, 1984.

Paul Johnson: *The National Trust Book of British Castles*; Weidenfeld and Nicolson and The National Trust, London, 1978.

Charles Oman: *Castles*; The Great Western Railway, London, 1926.

Somerset Fry, Plantagenet (1996): *Castles of Britain and Ireland*; Newton Abbot: David & Charles.

When comfort began to take precedence over security, many lords were given licence to crenellate their mansion houses. Acton Burnell in Shropshire is a typical example

Henry VIII led the last epoch in castle building, erecting a formidable set of defences across the south coast. They were usually of squat circular or cloverleaf construction, such as the castle at Deal in Kent
(photo courtesy of Ian Giles; www.iangilesphotos.co.uk)

Timeline

1066	William of Normandy defeats King Harold at the Battle of Hastings and becomes William I (William the Conqueror).
1068	Subjugation of the west; William builds the first motte-and-bailey castle at York.
1069	Subjugation of the north.
1070	Subjugation of the Welsh Marches.
1087	William dies and is succeeded by his third son, William II (Rufus).
1088	The rebellion of the barons; Bishop Odo is banished.
1100	Rufus is killed in the New Forest; Henry I, youngest son of the Conqueror, becomes king.
1120	Prince William, son of Henry I, is drowned in the *White Ship* disaster.
1135	Henry I dies of lampreys and his nephew Stephen seizes the throne which is claimed by Henry's daughter, the Empress Matilda, leading to civil war (Anarchy).
1141	Matilda briefly reigns after capturing the king at the Battle of Lincoln.
1153	The end of civil war.
1154	Henry II, son of Matilda, becomes king on the death of Stephen; the first Angevin king.
1171	Rhys ap Gruffydd, the Lord Rhys, Prince of Deheubarth, is made Justiciar of Wales.
1183	Henry's sons Richard and John, aided by their mother Eleanor, rebel against the king.
1189	Richard I (the Lionheart) succeeds his father after Henry's death.
1190	Richard sails to the Crusades; Jews persecuted at York.
1197	The Lord Rhys dies.
1199	Richard dies at the siege of Chalus; his brother John (Lackland) is made king.
1215	Magna Carta signed at Runnymede; civil war ensues.
1216	Louis, Dauphin of France, invades; John dies and is succeeded by nine-year old Henry III (Plantagenet); William Marshal, Earl of Pembroke becomes regent.
1227	Henry declares himself of age.
1240	Llywelyn ap Iorwerth (Llywelyn the Great), Prince of North Wales dies.
1263	Rebellion of Simon de Montfort; civil war.
1272	Henry dies and is succeeded by his son who becomes Edward I (Longshanks); Llywelyn ap Gruffydd (Llywelyn the Last) refuses homage to the king.
1277	Edward's first Welsh campaign; Llywelyn surrenders.
1282	Edward's second Welsh campaign; Llywelyn is killed near Builth Wells.
1283	Dafydd, Llywelyn's brother is executed; Edward's great Welsh castle building begins.
1307	Edward dies while marching on Scotland; his son becomes Edward II.
1312	The king's lover, Piers Gaveston, is murdered by the earls of Lancaster and Warwick.
1314	Edward is routed by Robert the Bruce at Bannockburn.
1322	The Earl of Lancaster is captured at Boroughbridge and executed.
1326	Edward is forced to abdicate by his wife Isabella and her lover, Roger Mortimer.
1327	Edward is horribly murdered at Berkeley Castle; his son succeeds him as Edward III.
1330	Edward captures and executes Mortimer, avenging his father's murder.
1337	The Hundred Years War.
1348–9	The Black Death kills many thousands in Britain and Europe.
1377	Richard II, son of the Black Prince, becomes king upon the death of his grandfather.
1381	Wat Tyler leads the Peasants' Revolt.
1399	John of Gaunt, Duke of Lancaster, third son of

	Edward III dies; Henry Bolingbroke, his son, becomes Henry IV after forcing Richard to abdicate.
1400	Richard dies in prison in Pontefract, probably murdered; uprising of Owain Glyndwr in Wales.
1403	Henry Percy, Earl of Northumberland, known as 'Hotspur', killed at Battle of Shrewsbury.
1408	Henry Percy, son of Hotspur, is killed at Bramham Moor.
1413	Henry V, son of Henry IV, becomes king.
1415	The Battle of Agincourt.
1422	The nine-month-old son of Henry V becomes Henry VI after the death of his father; England and France are ruled by the dukes of Bedford and Gloucester.
1453	The end of the Hundred Years War.
1455	Wars of the Roses between the houses of York and Lancaster.
1461	Edward IV, eldest son of Richard, Duke of York, is proclaimed king after defeating the Lancastrians at the Battle of Mortimer's Cross.
1464	Richard Neville, Earl of Warwick, known as the 'Kingmaker', crushes opposition to Edward; Henry VI is captured and imprisoned.
1470	Henry VI regains the throne with the help of Warwick.
1471	Henry is deposed and murdered; his son, Prince Edward, is killed at the battle of Tewkesbury.
1483	Edward V becomes king after the death of his father, but together with his brother Richard is taken to the Tower of London by his uncle Richard, Duke of Gloucester, and probably murdered; the duke assumes the Crown as Richard III.
1485	Richard is killed at the Battle of Bosworth, which marks the end of the Wars of the Roses; Henry Tudor, son of Edmund Tudor, is crowned Henry VII; first of the Tudor kings.
1499	Perkin Warbeck, pretender to the throne, executed.
1509	Henry dies and his second son becomes king as Henry VIII.
1536	Henry confirms his break with Rome after Pope's refusal to grant him a divorce; the Suppression Act closes small monasteries with an income of less than £200.
1536–37	Pilgrimage of Grace rebellion against the closure of religious houses in the North.
1537–40	The King's commissioners compel abbots to surrender the remaining abbeys and priories.
1540	The closure of Waltham Abbey in March completes the Dissolution of religious establishments in Britain.
1547	Edward VI, only child of Henry VIII and Jane Seymour, succeeds his father at age nine and rules with the aid of his uncle, the Duke of Somerset.
1553	Edward dies and is succeeded by the Catholic Mary I (Bloody Mary), eldest daughter of Henry VIII and Catherine of Aragon; Lady Jane Grey is placed on the throne by the Protestant faction but rules for only nine days; she is later executed.
1558	Elizabeth I, daughter of Henry VIII and Anne Boleyn, succeeds after the death of Mary.
1587	Mary, Queen of Scots, is executed for complicity in an attempt to restore the Catholic faith.
1603	James VI, King of Scotland since 1567, becomes James I of England upon the death of Elizabeth; the first Stuart king.
1625	The second son of James becomes king as Charles I.
1642	Civil War erupts between Parliamentarians and the Royalists.
1649	Charles is tried for treason and executed; Oliver Cromwell leads the Commonwealth for nine years until his death in 1658.
1660	Charles II becomes king after the restoration of the monarchy.

Glossary

Adulterine Unlicensed-castles built without Crown permission during King Stephen's reign
Arcade Row of arches supported by columns
Arrow loop Narrow opening for discharging arrows
Ashlar Worked stone with a flat surface, usually of regular shape and square edges
Bailey Castle courtyard enclosed by a wall; ward
Barbican Outer walled area blocking direct approach to the main gate
Barrel-vault Arched semi-cylindrical vault
Bartizan Overhanging corner turret
Bastion Projecting platform or low tower from which the area outside ramparts can be defended
Batter Inclined face of a wall; hence battered
Battlements Indented parapet with raised portions between; also called crenellations
Berm Level area separating a ditch from a bank
Brattice Timber tower or projecting wooden gallery; also known as hoarding
Buttery Storeroom for provisions
Buttress Projecting masonry on wall for additional strength
Capital Uppermost part of column or shaft, often decorated
Castellan Officer in charge of a castle; also known as a constable
Causeway Bank built across marshy ground with a footpath along the top
Chamfer Bevelled or mitred angle
Chevron Twelfth-century zigzag moulding
Concentric With two or more lines of defence, one inside the other
Constable Officer in charge of castle; castellan
Corbel Timber or stone projection to provide support
Crenellations Battlements with stone merlons interspersed with embrasures to permit defensive fire
Cross-wall Internal dividing wall in a great tower
Curtain wall Surrounding wall 'hung' between the towers of a castle
Donjon Principal tower; keep
Drawbridge Wooden bridge across a ditch or moat raised by ropes or chains
Dressings Worked stone used for corners and angles
Drum tower Low round tower built into a wall
Dungeon Jail, usually found in one of the towers
Embrasure Splayed opening in a parapet to permit defensive fire
Enceinte Circuit of outer ramparts
Finial Slender piece of stone used to decorate the tops of merlons and arches
Flanking tower Tower projecting from a corner of the keep or main stretch of curtain wall
Flying buttress A free-standing buttress linked to the building by part of an arch
Forebuilding Attached low building to guard the entrance to the keep
Gallery Long, narrow room or hallway
Garderobe Latrine, normally discharging into a cesspit or through an outer wall into a ditch
Gatehouse Strong defences protecting the main entrance
Gunport Opening in a wall through which a gun can be fired
Hall Principal living quarters
Hermit crab Medieval castle built inside an older castle
Herringbone Pattern of masonry inclined alternately to the left and right
Hoarding Timber tower or projecting wooden gallery; brattice

Hornwork Outer earthwork defences to protect vulnerable side
Keep Great tower; donjon
Keystone Central stone of an arch, sometimes carved
Knapped flint Flint dressed with a smooth side for building
Lancet High narrow window with a pointed head
Loop Narrow opening to discharge arrows or let in light; arrow loop
Machicolations Projecting stone galleries on the outside of towers or walls for dropping missiles
Mantlet Surrounding screen of masonry for other walls or defences
Merlon Section of battlements interspersed by embrasures; sometimes pierced with slits
Mine gallery Tunnel driven by besiegers under castle defences to bring about collapse
Moat Water-filled ditch often linked to a nearby river or stream
Motte Natural or artificially raised earth mound on which keep was built
Mullion Vertical division between lights of a window
Mural gallery Gallery constructed within the thickness of a wall
Murder hole Opening in the gatehouse ceiling to allow missiles to be dropped on an enemy below
Ogee Arch of continuous double-curve, convex and pointed above and concave below
Oriel Projecting window in a wall
Oubliette Dungeon reached by a trapdoor
Palisade Timber defensive screen
Parapet Rampart covering defenders from enemy observation and fire
Peel or Pele Tower stronghold without outer defences
Pilaster Shallow pier used to buttress a wall
Piscina Carved shallow basin in a wall niche near the altar for washing sacred vessels
Plinth Projecting base of a wall or column
Portcullis Heavy iron-shod wooden gate dropped vertically from groves to block the key passage
Postern Rear or secondary gate to a castle, often concealed
Quoins Dressed stones used to finish the external corners of buildings
Rampart Defensive stone or earth wall surrounding a castle
Revetment Retaining wall
Rib-vault Vault or arch supported by projecting bands of stone
Ring-work Circular earthwork of bank and ditch
Shell-keep Circular or oval wall surrounding inner portion of castle
Siege engine Stone-throwing device
Slighted Deliberately rendered indefensible by being wholly or partly demolished
Solar Upper living room on sunny side, offering privacy to the lord
Springing Level at which an arch or vault rises from its support
Squint Observation hole in a wall or room
Tracery Decorative intersecting rib-work in the upper part of window
Trebuchet War engine employing counterpoise
Turret Small round or polygonal tower
Vault Arched stone roof or ceiling, sometimes relieved by stone ribs
Wall-walk Passage along a castle wall
Ward Castle courtyard enclosed by a wall; bailey

English Heritage
National Trust
Independently owned

Norham
Etal
Dunstanburgh
Warkworth
Prudhoe
Brougham
Brough   Barnard Castle
Castle Bolton   Richmond
Middleham   Helmsley   Scarborough
Pickering
Clifford's Tower
Conisborough
Peveril
Beeston
Tutbury
Moreton Corbet   Ashby de la Zouch   Castle Rising
Kirby Muxloe   Castle Acre
Bungay
Clun   Stokesay   Framlingham
Ludlow   Kenilworth   Orford
Hedingham
Goodrich
Hadleigh
Farleigh   Rochester
Hungerford   Eynsford
Nunney   Knepp
Sherborne   Portchester   Bodium
Bramber   Pevensey
Tintagel   Okehampton
Launceston   Corfe
Restormel

12

Ashby de la Zouch

The Hastings Tower

When first erected and held by Hugh de Grentmeisnil, who accompanied William the Conqueror to England in 1066, Ascebi, as it was then called, was an unremarkable Norman manor house, built of timber and surrounded by a fence. Its location had little strategic value and no natural defences. After Philip Belmeis inherited the manor, the family flourished under the patronage of the Montgomerys of Shropshire, and some time around 1150 a more substantial house was built in stone to reflect the new status. Only the distinctive masonry of squared rubble with wide joints still visible in the walls of the hall and buttery would appear to date from that time. Philip died in 1160 without male heirs and the manor passed to a Breton nobleman, Alan la Zouch, who renamed it after his home in Brittany. When the manor passed to Sir William Mortimer in 1314, a new phase of building was begun. This involved the complete gutting of the inside – only the outer walls were retained – and the replacement of existing structures with a new single-storey hall, solar, buttery, and later a kitchen. Sir William assumed the name la Zouch and was created Baron Zouch of Ashby in 1323.

But Ashby de la Zouch attained real prominence only after 1464, when it was granted by Edward IV to William, Lord Hastings, his Lord Chamberlain,

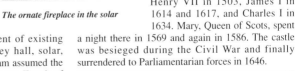

The ornate fireplace in the solar

who, ten years later, obtained a licence to crenellate. Hastings' principal addition was a formidable four-storey tower which, even in its ruined state, remains the most impressive part of the castle. Rectangular in plan with an extension on the north-east side, the tower was originally about 27.4m (90ft) high to its semi-octagonal turrets, and had unusually thick walls measuring 2.6m (nearly 9ft) at the base. There were no windows on the ground floor and access was via a small door protected by a portcullis. Hastings was also responsible for the large chapel and other domestic buildings, of which the solar, with its ornate fireplace and mullioned windows, is particularly noteworthy. He did not live long to enjoy his handiwork, as he was beheaded by Richard III in 1483. The castle, however, remained in the family and a string of royal visitors graced its halls, including Henry VII in 1503, James I in 1614 and 1617, and Charles I in 1634. Mary, Queen of Scots, spent a night there in 1569 and again in 1586. The castle was besieged during the Civil War and finally surrendered to Parliamentarian forces in 1646.

In Ashby de la Zouch, on A453 Tamworth Road, Leicestershire, England (OS reference SK 363167)
Tel: 01530 413343

Barnard Castle

This large and commanding fortress overlooks the River Tees, and it is from across the river that it should be viewed before embarking on its exploration. From within the town of the same name, the castle lies hidden and takes a while to find, the lack of directional signs making it somewhat difficult. Today's remains cover an extensive oblong enclosure, one side of which is bounded by a sheer cliff plunging towards the river, but the first castle was of a much more modest size and had a difficult gestation. The time leading up to its construction was marked by a lengthy dispute between the powerful bishops of Durham, the earls of Northumberland and the Crown over ownership of the land. This dispute was forcibly resolved in 1095, when William II seized the land from the Earl of Northumberland and granted it to Guy de Baliol, a supporter of his from Picardy in north-eastern France. Guy immediately constructed a small earthwork castle with a hall fortified by surrounding timber palisades. Nothing is left of this early castle, which was obliterated by the work of his nephew, Bernard de Baliol, who succeeded in 1215.

Bernard, together with his younger son Bernard de Baliol II, constructed what was one of the largest castles in the north of England. He also founded the town outside its walls that now bears his name. Covering 2.6 ha (6.5 acres), the castle was divided into four wards: the inner ward inside the smaller stone enclosure, the middle ward to the south, the town ward to the east, and the largest outer ward. The most interesting feature of Barnard is the cylindrical great tower, known as Baliol Tower, in the corner of the inner ward, which is the only part of the castle to survive almost complete. It is some 11m (36ft) in diameter and stands 12.2m (40ft) tall. Accommodation for the lord and lady were provided on the first and second floors, while the third gave access to the battlements, and the basement was used as a storeroom. Of note are the three arrow slits with 'fish-tail' bases that permitted covering fire to the outside base of the tower, and a spiral pattern on the ceiling. The mullioned oriel window in the remains of the great chamber affords a wonderful view over the river valley. Nothing is left of the adjacent kitchens, but there are remains of ovens in the bakehouse.

Surrounding the town ward are interesting remains of the Dovecote Tower, still with vestiges of nesting boxes, the north gatehouse with sewer pits for garderobes, and the Brackenbury Tower, all much ruined. The middle ward, also once known as 'Many Gates' for its three gates, provided accommodation for higher-ranking officers. It is separated from the outer ward by a rock-cut ditch. The outer ward, which housed the farm and includes the site of St Margaret's Chapel, is not open to visitors.

Barnard's position on the Scottish border left it open to attack. Like Norham, it was besieged by Alexander of Scotland in 1216, but both sieges proved unsuccessful. Except for a short period, Barnard Castle remained in the hands of the Baliols until 1296, when the family's most noted descendant, John de Baliol, was deposed as King of Scotland. Anthony Bek, Bishop of Durham, then

The view across the river

A mullioned oriel window

Baliol Tower

Near Barnard Castle town centre, County Durham, England (OS reference NZ 049165). Tel: 01833 638212

Points of interest
1. Remains of Headlam Tower and the sally port
2. Mortham Tower adjoining the kitchen block
3. Great hall and great chamber with oriel window and carved emblem of Richard III
4. Three-storey Round or Baliol Tower
5. Bakehouse with the remains of ovens
6. Dovecote Tower with nesting boxes
7. Brackenbury Tower with garderobe and the remains of the original stairs to the first floor
8. Fragments of the Constable Tower with rock-cut pits

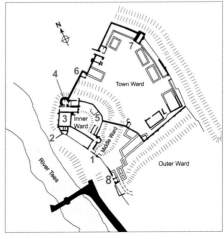

claimed it and its lands, but for only a short time. King Edward I granted it on his deathbed to Guy de Beauchamp, Earl of Warwick. It was held for a while by Richard, Duke of Gloucester, later Richard III, whose white boar emblem is carved on a window soffit in the west wall of the inner bailey. Alas, the soft sandstone has weathered so much it is largely unrecognisable. After the death of Richard, Barnard became dilapidated, but came into the spotlight again in 1536, when the constable, Robert Bowes, was forced to surrender the castle to rebels supporting the Pilgrimage of Grace. In 1569, it was besieged and surrendered again during the Rising of the North, which was intended to replace Elizabeth I with Mary, Queen of Scots.

Beeston Castle

The twin-towered gatehouse

Perched on a red sandstone crag 152m (500ft) high above the Cheshire Plain, Beeston Castle dominates the area for miles around and seems beyond the reach of mere mortals. Indeed, the climb through woodland paths towards the gatehouse is steep and tiring, and the outer walls and towers lull the visitor into a false sense of having arrived, when there is still much climbing to do. The first close-up view of the imposing twin-towered gatehouse, now approached by a slim modern bridge, makes it easy to imagine how impregnable this castle would have appeared to any would-be assailant once the drawbridge had been raised. The 360° vista from the central courtyard makes the long climb worthwhile, with views to the Pennines in the east, the Welsh hills to the west and the Wrekin to the south possible on a clear day. It is surprising to see another castle on an adjacent hill only a few miles away, but the medieval style Peckforton Castle, now a hotel, is a rather more modern construction, dating from 1844.

Beeston Castle was built by the powerful Ranulf de Blundeville, 6th Earl of Chester, to replicate the impregnable strongholds the Crusaders had encountered in the Holy Land. Construction started in 1225, but Ranulf died in 1232 before seeing it completed. His estate passed to his son John, but when he died just five years later without an heir, the earldom and still unfinished castle were seized by Henry III. It was used by him and his son, later

Edward I, as a base for their campaigns against the Welsh, assembling troops and storing supplies. As it was not required for residential accommodation, and no domestic buildings had been added in the inner ward, it is likely that temporary timber buildings for housing troops and supplies were erected on the slopes of the outer bailey. Edward I strengthened the castle with further walls and towers, but along with the other Cheshire castles, Beeston lost its strategic value after the Welsh had finally been conquered in the mid-1280s.

It later served as a refuge for Simon de Montfort after his defeat at Evesham in 1265. There is a popular belief that Richard II, hastening back from Ireland in 1399 to meet the threat posed by his usurping cousin Henry Bolingbroke, later to become Henry IV, dropped his treasure into the well at Beeston before falling into his enemies' hands. His personal fortune was said to have amounted to '100,000 marks in gold coin and 100,000 marks in other precious objects', but no coins, cups or jewellery have been found – though not for want of trying. This is perhaps not surprising, for the castle well was cut into the sandstone to a depth of 112m (367ft), an incredible feat for the time, and remains one of the deepest anywhere.

Abandoned and neglected, the castle fell into gradual decline until it was acquired by a local landowner, Sir Hugh Beeston of Beeston Hall at the beginning of the seventeenth century. Sir Hugh installed some of his farm workers within its walls, but on the outbreak of the Civil War in 1642 it was recommissioned. It fell first to the Parliamentarians and then to the Royalists, when a party of only eight soldiers managed to scale the north wall and tricked the eighty-strong garrison into surrender. The Royalists held the castle for two years, but it was inevitable that Cromwell would want to avenge this humiliation. After a siege in 1646 lasting four months, his troops succeeded in starving the Royalists into submission. A ferocious slighting left the castle in ruins.

What is left today is still an impressive sight. The lower curtain wall snaking along the more gently sloping side of the crag well away from the summit provided a formidable first line of defence. Although the wall and its seven projecting cylindrical towers are crumbling away, or in parts have virtually disappeared, and the eastern gatehouse is a mere fragment, it takes little effort to imagine what it must have looked like when first built. The same can be said for the strongly fortified upper enclosure, which is also badly decaying, although the twin towers of the gatehouse continue to stand like massive sentinels trying to bar progress.

W of Beeston village centre on minor road off A49 or A41, 18km (11 miles) SE of Chester, Cheshire, England (OS reference SJ 537593). Tel: 01829 260464

Points of interest
1. Outer gatehouse
2. Outer curtain walls with projecting towers
3. Well in the outer bailey
4. Massive twin-towered gatehouse to inner ward
5. Castle well, one of the deepest anywhere

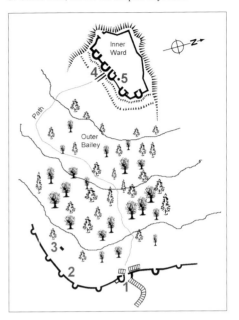

The castle well

Bodiam Castle

The approach to Bodiam Castle follows a similar course to that used in the Middle Ages and the astonishment at seeing a 'fairytale' castle set into high ground in the rolling Sussex countryside, its turreted towers reflected in sheets of water, is as powerful today as it must have been when it was first built. It is equally difficult to conceive that its setting in large part is anything but natural, with the impressive encircling moat, which covers 1.2 ha (3 acres), being retained against the slope of the hill by a dam of earth for nearly half its circumference. The castle itself looks formidable and the width of the moat was carefully designed to keep the walls outside the range of the cannons then being used. Access was via a causeway over the moat leading to a barbican which provided a first line of defence, while the last stretch to the main gate could be swept by the castle's own guns fired through keyhole ports in the twin towers. However, the dam to hold in the waters of the moat was a weak point and could easily have been breached, rendering the castle's defences less effective. But its defensive capabilities were never put to the test by French invaders, against whom Sir Edward Dalyngrigge had obtained a licence to crenellate it in 1385.

Sir Edward returned from the Hundred Years War with France in 1377 an immensely rich and powerful knight, and obtained the manor of Bodyham, as it was then called, through marriage to Elizabeth Wardieux. Bodyham, on the shores of the Rother and just 16km (10 miles) from the English Channel, took its name from an earlier Saxon settlement on the site. He used the threat of possible French invasion to apply to Richard II for a licence to crenellate, but this was probably driven more by a desire to show off his new-found wealth. Nevertheless, the licence was granted 'to our beloved and faithful Edward Dalyngrigge Knight, that he may strengthen with a wall of stone and lime, and may crenellate and may construct and make into a castle his manor house of Bodyham, near the sea … for the defence of the adjacent country, and the resistance to our enemies.' But rather than reinforcing his existing manor, Sir Edward selected a new site in a slightly more elevated position to construct an entirely new castle. The design is attributed to royal mason Henry Yevele, and building took until about 1388, at times using more than 1,000 men.

Little is known of the castle's early history, other than that after Sir Edward's death it was inherited by Sir John, and passed into the hands of the Lewknor family after the male line died out in 1470. It was ironic that, having been built to repel a French invasion, Bodiam faced its greatest danger from the English themselves. In 1483, Sir Thomas Lewknor was implicated in plots against Richard III, who compelled the Earl of Surrey to regain 'Bodyham which the rebels have seized'. But the expected battle never materialised and the castle appears to have been surrendered without a fight. Suggestions that it was slighted by Parliamentarians in 1644 during the Civil War, when it was owned by Sir John Tufton, have not been proven. It is more likely that it was already ruinous by then.

The visitor today approaches the main gate in a straight line, although originally the wooden bridge ran from the western side to the octagonal island before turning right towards a barbican tower and

The castle and moat

Coats of arms on the gatehouse

thence to the main gatehouse. The gatehouse is framed by two battlemented towers and still has its iron-shod portcullis. Inside, a central courtyard is surrounded by the domestic buildings constructed against the outer walls. Even in its ruinous state, it is clear that accommodation was extremely comfortable, if not luxurious, especially Dalyngrigge's private chambers and chapel on the eastern side of the courtyard, which had direct access to the great hall. As to the outside, the magnificent setting. particularly when the mellow stone turrets rise to meet the setting sun at the same time mirrored in the shimmering waters, makes Bodiam one of the most photographed castles in the land.

Close to Bodiam village, 6km (4 miles) SE of Hawkhurst, Kent, England (OS reference TQ 785256). Tel: 01580 830436

The chapel window

The corner tower with household apartments

Points of interest
1. Remains of the barbican
2. Main gatehouse with twin towers and portcullis
3. NE tower with lodgings
4. Chapel with sacristy and closet above
5. Private chambers and privy tower
6. SE tower with lodgings
7. Great Hall
8. Postern gate
9. SW tower with vaulted chamber and well in basement
10. NW tower with lodgings

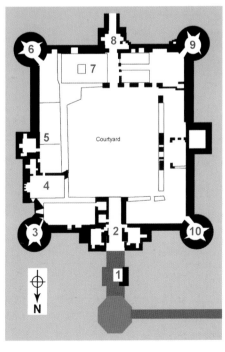

Bramber and Knepp Castles

The west wall of the keep with some surviving Caen stone facing

A fragment of the keep is all that remains of Knepp

Only the chattering of woodland birds now breaks the silence on the steep chalk outcrop above the ancient Sussex village of Bramber, where once stood a proud fortress, built around 1080 by the Norman knight William de Braose, an ally of William the Conqueror. Alas little is left bar the towering west wall of the gatehouse keep, which rises almost vertically some 17m (56ft) into the air and continues to defy the laws of gravity, especially considering that it was built from a mixture of flint, soft local limestone and lumps of chalk. The other three sides have fallen down long ago, with enormous blocks of flint work still lying in the ditch that surrounds the castle site. On the face of the tower, some of the Caen stone imported from Normandy has survived local plundering. Fragments of the formidable curtain wall also survive, as does the original motte, now covered by mature trees. Although de Braose was faced with the envy of his fellow lords at Arundel and Lewes, Bramber Castle was never attacked or besieged, but was allowed to fall into ruin after the last de Braose died in 1394.

William the Conqueror presented the Rape of Bramber to William de Braose in 1070. The Rape was a wide swathe of land extending from the coast of Shoreham as far as the Surrey border near Crawley, and was soon coveted by his neighbours.

To protect himself from possible attacks, William set about building a wooden castle in 1073, which was soon replaced by stone defences, incorporating a gatehouse keep. A deep ditch was dug around the site, except in the east where a tributary of the Adur formed a natural safeguard. At that time, the Adur was fully navigable up to Bramber, which made it relatively easy to bring supplies into the port below the castle. St Nicholas' Church was also built around 1073 to serve as the castle chapel and is still standing.

Around the same time, William de Braose built a second castle Knepp, nearby, of which only a fragment of wall from the keep survives on a shallow mound and can be seen from the road. Both castles were seized by King John around 1212 after the third William de Braose, grandson of the castles' builder, was implicated in the barons' revolt. William's wife and son were imprisoned in a dungeon at Windsor and starved to death. William himself escaped, disguised as a beggar, and fled to France. King John, Queen Isabella and Henry III all visited Knepp, and John also stayed at Bramber.

On W of Bramber village off A283, 8km (5 miles) north of Shoreham (TQ 185107) and N of Worthing on A24 W of West Grinstead village, West Sussex, England (TQ 163209). Unattended

Brough Castle

This remote castle, surrounded by a dry ditch, stands on a prominent knoll, and the views over the rolling Cumbrian hills and valleys dotted with farmsteads make it well worth the long trek. A narrow footpath leads from the village through a farmyard to the ruins, which are situated in the southern corner of a rectangular Roman fort, called Verteris, the remains of which can still be made out. Brough was one of the earliest castles to be built in stone. Being in the frontline of the defensive barrier against the Scots, it suffered accordingly. William II raised it in 1092 after retaking Westmorland, and there is evidence that it was at least partly built in stone, with fragments of an early tower underlying the present keep. The first work was a roughly triangular enclosure and part of the original curtain wall on the north side has characteristic Norman herringbone masonry. In 1136, it was seized by the Scots, who were only ousted in 1157, when it was granted by Henry II to Hugh de Morville. The castle's defensive strength was tested again and found wanting in 1174, when it was attacked and burned by the Scottish king, William the Lion. Theobald de Valoignes rebuilt the destroyed keep in 1179. King John gave the castle to his henchman, Robert de Vieuxpont, who built a gatehouse and great hall, which later collapsed.

Brough passed to Robert Clifford through marriage in 1268, at which time the castle was already much neglected and decayed. Roger made extensive repairs in about 1300 and erected a great hall and a round tower, now known as Clifford's Tower. He also strengthened the curtain wall against renewed threats from Scottish raiders. The castle remained a major residence for the Cliffords until 1521, when it was badly damaged by fire during a 'Great Christmas' held by Henry Clifford. Lady Anne Clifford rebuilt it in 1659–63, but after her

The remains of the tower keep

death in 1676 much of the stone was taken for use elsewhere. The most prominent surviving feature is the rectangular keep, four storeys high and built of sandstone-dressed rubble, with pilaster buttresses on the angles and mid-wall on the north and south walls. Patches of plasterwork can still be seen on the inside of the keep. Clifford's Tower and the adjacent great hall and other domestic buildings still stand to a fair height, although their walls are now much ruined. Only one room is still largely intact.

S of Brough town centre, 13km (8 miles) SE of Appleby, Cumbria, England (OS reference NY 791141). Unattended

The south side of castle

Brougham Castle

The red sandstone ruins of Broughham Castle on the banks of the River Eamont, surrounded by open farmland dotted with mature trees, stand out from their green enclosure as a glorious reminder of an often turbulent past. Built on only a slight rise, it had few natural defences except for the small river, and it comes as no surprise that the marauding Scots found it rather easy to penetrate. Yet its strategic location had been recognised hundreds of years before by the Romans, who established the fort of Brocavum to the south of the present castle at the junction of two major Roman roads opening up the Cumbrian hinterland. Like the medieval fortress, it too was sited to guard the river crossing. Remains of the fort can still be seen outside the castle walls.

The castle's origin is somewhat vague, but it is thought to have been raised by Hugh de Morville in 1070 during the reign of Henry II. The substantial square tower, erected on the Roman earthworks and built of sandstone rubble finished with ashlar stone, dates from that period and has

The carved stone, 'Thys made Roger' over the gatehouse

survived in fine shape. The timber palisade was not replaced by a stone curtain until the time of Robert de Vieuxpont, who was granted the castle by King John in 1203. De Vieuxpont also added a large rectangular hall, of which now only the foundations remain, and a forebuilding to the tower. After his death at the Battle of Evesham in 1228, where he

supported Simon de Montfort, the castle suffered severe neglect. In 1268, it passed to Robert Clifford, whose father had become Lord of Brougham when he married Robert Vieuxpont's daughter, Isabella.

The keep was originally three storeys high, but Robert Clifford added a top storey of better quality with a private apartment and chapel late in the thirteenth Century. Pilaster angle buttresses provide strengthening on three sides away from the forebuilding, and another noticeable feature is a projecting part of the upper floor, which is still supported on the western edge by carved corbels. The small private chapel can be recognised and retains a fine vaulted roof and fragments of a carved piscina. A Roman tombstone has been built into the ceiling of a wall passage, with its Latin inscription partially legible. Its translates as '*To the spirits of the departed; Tittus M – lived thirty-two years more or less. M –, his brother set up this inscription.*' A spiral staircase and wall passages lead to the top of the tower, from where there is a fine view over the surrounding countryside. Robert was also responsible for the two gatehouses with portcullises which enclosed an inner ward, and another tower, now known as the Tower of the League, in the south-west corner, which were designed to provide extra protection against the rampant Scots. The inner gatehouse has an

The castle from across the river

The tower keep

interesting staircase that leads from the private rooms on the first floor to the postern gate and thence to the riverbank, making it possible for the lord to escape unseen. Robert's grandson, Roger, added a great hall in the 1380s, and the original carved stone over the entrance, which reads 'Thys made Roger', is now to be found in the gatehouse wall. Nothing is left of the service range, but the accommodation blocks for troops stand to a good height.

In 1388 Brougham was virtually destroyed by the Scots and left to decay until about 1525, when reconstruction was put in hand by George Clifford, Earl of Cumberland. However, Oliver Cromwell showed no mercy in the Civil War, demolishing the castle in 1648. Enter the ageing and eccentric Lady Anne Clifford, who had inherited Brougham in 1643

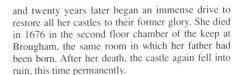

The three-arched sedilia

and twenty years later began an immense drive to restore all her castles to their former glory. She died in 1676 in the second floor chamber of the keep at Brougham, the same room in which her father had been born. After her death, the castle again fell into ruin, this time permanently.

On minor road off A66, 2.5km (1.5 miles) SE of Penrith, Cumbria, England (OS reference NY 537290). Tel: 01768 862488.

Points of interest
1. Outer Gatehouse
2. Gatehouse with stairs to postern gate
3. Tower Keep with hall
4. Covered passage to chapel
5. Chapel with three-arched sedilia
6. Accommodation blocks for castle guards
7. Tower of the League

The vaulted gatehouse passage

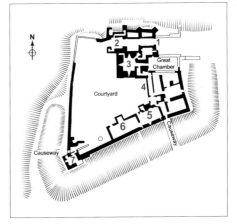

Bungay Castle

The twin-towered gatehouse

Only fragments of masonry from the Norman keep and a later, more complete gatehouse now give an indication of what was once a formidable stronghold of the notorious Hugh Bigod (the Bold), who proved a constant irritant to successive monarchs in the twelfth Century. Although Bungay was later eclipsed by the Bigods' other castle at Framlingham, it was during a siege of the latter by King Henry II in 1174 that Hugh Bigod was said to have declared: 'Were I in my castle of Bungaye above the water of Waveney, I would ne care a button for the king of Cockney and all his meiny [armed forces].' Although largely dismantled and decayed, Bungay Castle remains an attractive landmark in the Suffolk town of the same name, built on high ground and encircled by the River Waveney looping around two sides. As a result, the castle occupied a strong defensive position, with more vulnerable aspects protected by ramparts and ditches.

Bigod's castle, the building of which is thought to have commenced in 1165, is likely to have been preceded by an earlier fortification to guard against Danish raiders. After the Norman Conquest, the site was acquired by William de Noyers, who may have raised a motte and bailey type castle as protection against hostile Saxon tribes. In 1103, King Henry I bestowed Bungay on Roger Bigod, but after his early death it came into the hands of his younger son Hugh, who established a dominant position among the barons of East Anglia and frequently took up arms against the reigning monarch. When King Stephen marched on Bungay in 1140 to put down the rebellious baron, Hugh decided that negotiation was the better part of valour, and was rewarded with the title of Earl of Norfolk.

On the accession of Henry II in 1154, he was deprived of both Bungay and Framlingham, but had them returned to him in 1163. This proved an ill-judged decision, for in 1173 he joined forces with Henry II's son, the Earl of Leicester, in yet another, ultimately futile, rebellion. But when the king mustered a large army against him, Hugh was forced to capitulate and was branded a traitor. A mine gallery, still visible today, was cut under the foundations of the keep, but after paying a fine of 1,000 marks, Hugh was able to save Bungay from destruction. After his death in Syria in 1178, Bungay fell into disuse, and it was not until Roger Bigod, the 5th earl, obtained a licence to crenellate, that Bungay was revived. Roger is credited with the erection of the gatehouse and curtain walls encircling the original castle mound in 1294. Like his more illustrious ancestor, Roger took up arms against the monarch, but he died soon after building was completed in 1297. Since he left no heir, Bungay Castle devolved to the Crown and in 1312 was bestowed by Edward II to his brother Thomas de Brotherton, Earl Marshall of England. After several more changes it passed to the Howards, dukes of Norfolk, in 1483, but already a hundred years before, it had been described as 'old and ruinous and worth nothing a year.'

The extent of the castle can be gauged by the

Sparse fragments of the keep

separately sited keep and the remnants of the curtain walls enclosing the inner bailey. Grass now grows where the great hall stood alongside the northern wall, traces of which survive, although they are now largely obscured by dense hedges and undergrowth. The most prominent feature is the imposing gatehouse. Its massive twin towers, 6.5m (21ft) in diameter, still stand to a good height, and were built of flint and sandstone rubble from the upper part of the keep. Some one-third of the estimated original height of 11.5m (38ft) has been faced with ashlar. Access to the gatehouse would have been via a wooden bridge over the ditch in front. The 21m (70ft) square keep, with walls 5.5m (18ft) thick on three sides and 7m (23ft) at the northern end, would have stood to a height of at least 30m (100ft). Because most of the stone was plundered, little has been learned of its interior configuration, although more evidence exists of the three-storey forebuilding, which had a prison in the basement, and possibly a chapel in the upper chamber.

A brick archway

In town of Bungay, Suffolk, England (OS reference TM 336896). Tel: 01986 896156

Points of interest
1. Remains of curtain wall around the keep
2. Bridge pit with grooves for the balancing weight of the bridge
3. Gatehouse with semicircular twin towers open at the rear
4. Low fragments of the Norman Keep
5. Forebuilding with a prison in the basement, cesspit and latrine
6. Mine gallery

St Mary's Church from the castle

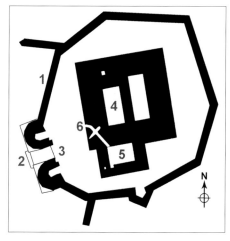

Castle Acre

The pretty Norfolk village of Castle Acre, which lies on the ancient Peddars Way, an important Roman track to the north Norfolk coast, is dominated by its castle at one end, and the magnificent remains of a Cluniac priory at the other. Once itself a fortified town, the village and its ruins are inextricably linked with the earls of Surrey, for many generations among the wealthiest and most powerful of Norman lords. Castle Acre was the focal point of their Norfolk estates. William de Warenne supported William the Conqueror at the Battle of Hastings and was richly rewarded with lands in over a dozen counties. He quickly set about building castles to protect his lands, and although Lewes in Sussex remained the chief seat, Castle Acre played an important role in the affairs of the family and the state. Henry III stayed there several times, while the Earl also entertained Edward I there on a number of occasions between 1292 and 1301. The earliest structure, probably built in around 1170, was a two-storey residential block surrounded by a ditch and bank, but this was rebuilt into a massive keep in the middle of the following century. A flint-faced crenellated curtain wall with a wall-walk was constructed to surround the upper ward. The larger, lower ward was also strengthened for defensive purposes. After the end of the direct line of the de Warennes in 1347, the castle fell into disuse and changed hands many times. Some repairs were undertaken in 1615 when it was in the hands of the Chief Justice, Sir Edward Coke, but no records exist of what this work may have entailed.

Few of the castle's remains extend much above ground today, but the site nevertheless impresses with the extensive and formidable earthworks raised to boost the defensive capabilities of the gently rising ground on which it stands. After passing through the bailey gate, the former northern gateway of the town, the much ruined west gate, with scant evidence of two drum towers, gives access to the grassed lower ward. This is notable only for the outline of two buildings thought to have been the great hall and chapel. Only part of a wall remains of the east gate, and little more reaches above ground on the upper ward. What remains of the keep lies in a hollow, which is the result of the surrounding bank being raised on two separate occasions. Parts of the curtain wall survive to almost full height.

NE end of Castle Acre village, 8km (5 miles) N of Swaffham, Norfolk, England (OS reference TF 819152). Tel: 01760 755394

The upper ward defences

The remains of the keep

Castle Bolton

The castle, high above Wensleydale

Occupying a prominent position on rising ground overlooking Wensleydale on the edge of the Yorkshire Dales National Park, Castle Bolton dominates its surroundings for a fair distance. Although now partly ruined, the large quadrangular fortified mansion stands as a proud monument to one of the more interesting families of medieval England. It is still owned by Lord Bolton, a descendant of the castle's builder Sir Richard le Scrope, 1st Lord of Bolton and Lord Chancellor of England. Sir Richard started work on his new house, which was to reflect the family's great wealth, rank and standing in the community, in 1378, and a year later received a licence to crenellate from Richard II. It took eighteen years to complete and cost some £12,000, an enormous sum for the time. While the emphasis was on lavish and extensive residential accommodation, with three-storey ranges built into the walls around a rectangular courtyard, the castle was also provided with an effective defensive system. The gate on the east wall still retains its double portcullises at each end, but if the gate had been breached, attackers would have been faced by crossfire from fireloops in the inner walls and machicolations on the corner towers, which commanded every angle of the courtyard. The four doorways and narrow staircases in the corners, which lead to the upper rooms, were additionally protected by portcullises.

Although the castle is now partly ruined, it is possible to explore many of its halls and galleries, their original 600-year old beams still intact. The great hall on the first level contrasts sharply with the dank dungeon down below, and a climb to the top of one of the towers rewards the visitor with fine views over the dale. But the top attraction is the chamber where the unfortunate Mary, Queen of Scots, was held prisoner after fleeing to England in summer 1568, following her defeat at the Battle of Langside. In January 1569, during a heavy snowstorm, she was transferred to Tutbury Castle on the orders of Elizabeth I, who was probably concerned that her gaoler Sir Henry Scrope was the brother-in-law of the Duke of Norfolk, who had designs on the throne by marrying Mary. During the Civil War, Bolton was strongly defended for the king, but was surrendered on honourable terms in 1645. It was ordered by parliament to be 'rendered untenable' in 1647. In the sixteenth century, Sir Francis Knollys described Bolton as having the highest walls of any house he had seen, and that is just how it looks today.

Off A684 in Castle Bolton village, 8km (5 miles) W of Leyburn, North Yorkshire, England (OS reference SE 034918). Tel: 01969 623981.
Web: www.boltoncastle.co.uk

The west view

Castle Rising

The castle keep surrounded by massive earthworks

The squat rectangular flint keep, almost hidden behind massive double defensive earthworks which take up an area of some 5 ha (12 acres), is now virtually all that remains of this East Anglian fortress. The curtain wall that stretched along the top of the huge embankment has all but vanished. Only a few fragmented sections survive today and the gatehouse, a rectangular tower at the top of the inner bailey, also stands much reduced. At the northern end, the foundations of a Norman chapel of the eleventh century, raised before the keep, which itself dates from about 1138, can still be recognised. But the richly decorated great keep, which is in a fine state of preservation, holds more than enough fascination to warrant a visit to this sleepy rural outpost of Britain. The sides, which measure 24m × 20.7m (79ft × 68ft) are greater than the height, which reaches 15.2m (50ft) today, accentuate its solid bulk. The parapets and the tops of the corner turrets, now gone, would have increased the height a little more, but would have made little difference to its overall appearance.

Yet the pilaster buttresses clasping the corner turrets and the three slimmer pilasters along three walls, together with rich Norman carved and arcaded stonework, make this one of the most attractive keeps in the country. The first-floor main entrance is protected by a forebuilding with its own corner buttresses, of the same height as the tower. Adjoining the forebuilding is a stout wall, which hides a two-flight staircase that rises beyond an arched gateway to the double-height Great Hall and Great Chamber on the first floor. Notable is the elegant blind arcading along the top of the wall and the corbelled frieze and stone decorations above the Norman arch. An off-centre cross-wall divides the keep from top to bottom. Both the cross-wall and external walls have a number of rooms and passages, including a private chapel and a vaulted kitchen with a great circular hearth and an oven. An interesting feature is a small mural passage, which was carved out of the masonry at a much later date.

Castle Rising will always be associated with Queen Isabella, the 'She Wolf of France', who was banished to the castle after the gruesome murder of her husband, Edward II, at Berkeley Castle, aided and abetted by her lover Roger Mortimer. After governing the country during the minority of her son, Edward III, Isabella was confined to luxurious imprisonment at Castle Rising in 1329, but not before the new king had Mortimer executed. Isabella remained here for nearly thirty years until her death in 1358, receiving four visits from her son and being allowed out on infrequent journeys only with his permission. This was only one important historic interlude in the fascinating life of the castle. It was built by William d'Albini soon after his marriage in 1138 to the widow of Henry I, Queen Alice of Louvain, which conferred on William the earldoms of Lincoln and Sussex. The establishment of a mint in 1140, which produced coins for several years, was an interesting addition to the new castle. The d'Albini family retained ownership for the next 200 years until, in 1337, Edward III granted the castle

28

and manor to his eldest son, Edward the Black Prince, along with the newly created Duchy of Cornwall. Ownership took effect only from the death of Queen Isabella. Edward spent much money strengthening the fortifications and made Castle Rising battle-ready, in case of a landing by the French, which never came.

Following his early death in 1376, the castle changed hands several times. A peaceful period ensued until 1461, when it was put on alert during the Wars of the Roses between the houses of York and Lancaster, but suffered no siege. Richard III, then Duke of Gloucester, stayed at Castle Rising in 1469 accompanying Henry IV. Thomas Howard, Duke of Norfolk, obtained the manor form Henry VIII in 1544, but carried out little maintenance, so that it slowly decayed. A survey in 1572 suggested to Elizabeth I that it would cost £2,000 to repair the castle, but added that 'if the same castle should be taken downe and sold for benefitt, it is so greatlie decaied as the same will not yeald above one hundred marks'.

In Castle Rising village off A149, 6km (4 miles) NE of King's Lynn, Norfolk, England (OS reference TF 666246). Tel: 01553 631330

Stone decorations above the Norman arch

A tiled infill to a doorway

A small mural passage

Points of interest
1. Remains of the rectangular gatehouse to the inner bailey
2. Foundations of the eleventh Century church
3. Wall with blind arcading alongside the forebuilding
4. Norman arch with extensive stone decorations above
5. Great keep with the great hall and chapel

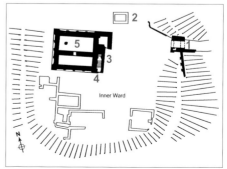

Clifford's Tower

Surrounded by a car park and set atop a man-made mound in the midst of town houses in the heart of York, Clifford's Tower still exudes an aura of dominance, although its cracked and mellow walls hide a gruesome past. The 18.3m (60ft) high mound was built by William the Conqueror as part of a line of castles to control his northern lands, and was originally topped by a wooden tower and surrounded by a fortified bailey. The castle gained notoriety when during anti-Semitic riots in 1190, 150 'Jews of York' either committed suicide in the burning tower or were massacred as they emerged from it pleading for mercy. Resentment against the Jewish population began to flare up under Henry II, whose extensive castle building programme caused him to borrow heavily from the Jews in York and forced him to impose heavy taxes on the population as a consequence. When leading Jews attended the coronation of Richard the Lionheart in 1189, it set off a series of riots, which spread through the land. In March 1190, the York Jews sought refuge in the tower, but when an enraged local crowd wheeled heavy siege equipment up the mound, their position became hopeless. In springtime, the mound is ablaze with yellow daffodils planted to commemorate this black day in the annals of this historic city.

In 1244, Henry III visited York and commissioned the reconstruction of the burnt-out tower in limestone. The shape of the new tower was of an unusual quatrefoil shape, with a rectangular forebuilding, strengthened with a portcullis and heavy entrance doors, added between two of the curves. A curtain wall incorporating two gateways and five towers was built around the large bailey, which assumed great importance in the reign of Edward I, who accommodated the royal courts and the exchequer in it. Unfortunately, nothing has survived of those structures. The Jews had once again become prosperous in York and elsewhere, but in 1290, Edward I declared usury (the loan of money at exorbitant interest rates) illegal and expelled all Jews from the kingdom. The castle was abandoned in the mid-fourteenth century and decayed rather badly, but was once again fortified and garrisoned by the king during the Civil War, until it was surrendered in 1644. A fire in 1684 caused further damage, leaving today's empty shell. Alongside the royal arms above the entrance are those of Roger de Clifford, after whom the tower is named. He was a Lancastrian leader who was hanged in chains from the top of the ramparts in 1332. A wonderful view over the city makes a climb to the wall-walk a must.

In Clifford Street, York, North Yorkshire, England (OS reference SE 605515). Tel: 01904 646940

The royal Clifford arms above the entrance

The tower sitting atop a large man-made motte

Clun Castle

The keep, built into the sloping side of the motte

Lying on the edge of the Forest of Clun, within a stone's throw of Offa's Dyke, Clun Castle was one of the many Norman strongholds built along the Welsh Marches. While little is now left standing, apart from the still substantial remains of the keep and a few fragments of the curtain wall with three bastions, Clun is noteworthy for the curious construction of its 24.3m (80ft) high keep. Rather than sitting atop the hill, it has been cut into the side, with most of its support at the level of the ditch. Two of its five stories were thus sited below the top of the curtain wall. It is thought that the motte was too weak to take this massive structure, forcing the builder to take the foundations to the bedrock lower down. This unique feature alone makes a visit worthwhile, but the arrangement of the ditch cut into the lower knoll and the sharply scarped sides towards the river, the whole complex enclosing two strongly defended baileys, also add to the experience of what once was a quite formidable stronghold.

The interior of the keep

Clun Castle was built around 1140–50 by Robert de Say, a follower of Earl Roger of Montgomery, as part of a marcher lordship known as the Honour of Clun. It was erected on the highest of three knolls, surrounded on three sides by the snaking River Clun. The stone keep and curtain wall were erected following the destruction of the timber defences after a siege by the Lord Rhys in 1196, and are believed to have been the work of the FitzAlans, lords of Oswestry, who had acquired Clun through marriage. The castle is said to have seen further action during the Barons' War in 1215, but suffered little damage. It would appear that after John FitzAlan became Earl of Arundel and the greatest landowner in Sussex in 1243, the family's castles in the Welsh Marches became rather neglected. As the smallest, Clun probably suffered more than most, and after the earl's death in 1272, a subsequent survey reported that the tower roof and the bridge connecting the castle with the outer bailey 'were in need of repair'. Some remedial work may have been carried out by the time Owain Glyndwr attacked the castle in 1404, but it was left to decay thereafter. When Leland passed by in around 1540, he found Clun 'somewhat ruinous, though it hath been strong and well builded'. In 1580, Clun came into the possession of the Howards, dukes of Norfolk, but soon became Crown property and James I gave it to the Earl of Northampton in 1604. Its ruinous state notwithstanding, it was slighted by Parliamentarians in 1646.

Off B4368 in Clun village, Shropshire, England (OS reference SO 298809). Unattended

Conisbrough Castle

The castle from the south-west

The pale tower keep rising from high ground above the river Don in Conisbrough serves as an unexpected landmark in the industrial heartland of South Yorkshire. Heavy with royal connections and for a long time in the hands of the earls de Warenne, the stone castle is believed to have replaced an earlier motte-and-bailey castle, built around 1070 by William, the first Earl de Warenne and son-in-law of William the Conqueror. The well-preserved, 27.5m (90ft) high keep dates from about 1180, and was apparently designed by the 5th Earl, the illegitimate half-brother of Henry II, Hamelin Plantagenet, who held the earldom from 1163 until his death in 1202. The keep, constructed from pale ashlar limestone, is considered to be the finest Norman keep in the country. It is unusual in being of cylindrical construction inside and out, strengthened by six huge, semi-hexagonal full-height buttresses splayed outwards at the base for additional support. It has a vaulted basement, three floors and a wall-walk at roof level, with the Lord's Hall on the top floor notable for a handsome fireplace. There is also a small chapel built into one of the buttresses, which retains fragments of Norman decoration.

It is assumed that the stone curtain walls were constructed soon after the keep, with the stone buildings probably added by Hamelin's son William. Within this enclosure there is much of interest to encourage exploration. The remains of the great hall retain some of the earliest hooded fireplaces known in England, while parts of an oven and two large cooking fires have survived in the adjacent kitchen and bakehouse. Much conjecture exists about a large stone trough in the service area, whose purpose is unknown, although its use as a urinal has been suggested. At the main entrance to the castle, the double-angle barbican is a clever feature designed to deny attackers a direct approach to the gate leading to the inner ward.

After the death of William in 1239, the castle passed to John, son of his second wife Maud, the widow of Hugh Bigod, Earl of Norfolk. During his tenure, which lasted until his death in 1304, records tell of the imprisonment of men and women, with one of the constables at the castle, Richard de Heydon, charged with 'devilish and innumerable oppressions'. John left no heir, as his only son William was killed at a tournament in Guildford in 1286, and he was succeeded by his grandson John. An arranged marriage to Joan de Barr, granddaughter of Edward I, proved unhappy and childless, and efforts to divorce his wife were thwarted by Thomas, Earl of Lancaster. John retaliated by abducting Lancaster's wife, Alice, upon which Lancaster promptly seized Conisbrough in 1317. It was a short-lived victory, for in 1322, Thomas was executed for treason.

Edward II then held the castle until he returned it to John four years later, although it reverted to the Crown on his death in 1347. As he left no heir, John was the 8th and last Earl de Warenne. Edward III conferred the estate on his youngest son, Edmund Langley, whose tenure lasted until 1402, when he was succeeded by his remaining son, Edward, Duke of Albemarle, who alas died at Agincourt in 1415. The castle eventually passed to the son of Richard, Duke of York, later Edward IV. By that time, the castle already seems to have suffered neglect, and a

The inner ward from the keep

survey by Henry VIII's commissioners recorded in 1537 that much of the gatehouse, the bridge and the walling had fallen, leaving the castle indefensible and leading to its decommissioning. The remains were granted to the Carey family, who held it for a long period. It escaped slighting during the Civil War, probably because of its poor state.

Three monarchs stayed at Conisbrough: King John, nephew of Hamelin in 1201, Edward II in 1322, and Edward IV. In more recent times, the castle was made famous by Sir Walter Scott's novel, Ivanhoe. Although it seems empty once visitors have departed, it is said to have not just one ghost, but several, although no evidence or suggestions have been advanced as to who these spectral wanderers at night may have been in life.

NE of Conisbrough town centre off A630, 7km (4.5 miles) SW of Doncaster, South Yorkshire, England (OS reference SK 515989). Tel: 01709 863329. Web: www.conisbroughcastle.org.uk

Points of interest
1. Barbican with a double-angle passage
2. Remains of the gatehouse
3. Tower keep with vaulted basement, garderobes, a small chapel and the Lord's Hall with fireplace
4. Great hall with hooded fireplaces, the earliest known in England
5. West range accommodation block
6. Kitchen and bakehouse with the remains of an oven and two large cooking fires
7. Service area with large stone trough, whose purpose is unknown

The cylindrical keep, with full-height buttresses

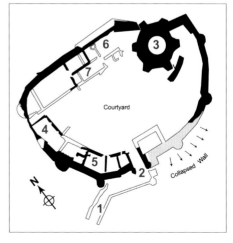

Corfe Castle

Commanding a natural gap in the hills cutting through the Isle of Purbeck peninsula, the splendid ruins of Corfe Castle cling desperately to an isolated green hillock high above the village, with the defiant King's Tower still thrusting its broken walls upwards. Corfe's rugged splendour, be it in the soft morning light, broodingly dark on stormy days or like smouldering embers under the setting sun, has no equal and seems an eternal presence not diminished by the passing of time. It should be remembered that only treachery and the ruthless savagery of the Parliamentarians were able destroy a fortress built more than 1,000 years ago to guard against invaders from the sea. But this was only the final chapter in a

The view from the south

long history, punctuated by heroic interludes and dastardly deeds. Exactly when it was built has been lost in the mists of time, but it is known that the Saxon King Edgar resided at Corfe (the Anglo-Saxon word for 'gap') and was probably responsible for constructing the keep.

Blood was first spilt in 978 when the young King Edward was murdered at the castle gates at the instigation of his stepmother Elfrida, Edgar's widow, determined to get his half-brother Ethelred 'The Unready' on the throne of England. The tragic event was recorded in the *Anglo-Saxon Chronicle* with the words, 'There has not been 'mid Angles a worse deed done than this was since they first Britain-land sought. Men had him murdered, but God him glorified. He was in life an earthly king; he is now after death a heavenly saint ...' Edward the Martyr was canonised and lies buried at Shaftesbury Abbey. Legend has it that when Elfrida attempted to follow the funeral procession from Wareham to Shaftesbury, the horse she rode refused to move, as did others she tried. Elfrida ended her days as a nun in an attempt to atone for her crime.

Following the Norman Conquest in 1066, the castle was developed, with the outer timber palisades replaced by impressive stone fortifications which followed the natural slopes of the knoll. During the wars of the Anarchy in the twelfth Century, King Stephen, grandson of William the Conqueror, unsuccessfully besieged Corfe, which was then held by Henry I's daughter Matilda. Around 1200, the castle became one of King John's favourite places of residence and while he greatly extended the castle, lavishing more than £1,400 mostly on the Gloriette,

Corfe guarding the approach from the sea

Edward the Martyr's Gate

The King's Tower

an apartment block next to the King's Tower, he also made it the scene of well-documented acts of brutality. He used it as his state prison and is said to have starved to death twenty-two French noblemen for backing his nephew's claim to the throne, and strung up a local prophet, Peter the Hermit, who had rather unwisely, forecast the King's downfall in 1212. He was dragged on a hurdle to Wareham and back, and was then hanged on a gallows.

Corfe Castle survived the War of the Roses in the fifteenth century, and having enjoyed a period of relative stability was sold in 1572 by Queen Elizabeth I to Sir Christopher Hatton, who was to become Lord Chancellor. Sir Christopher restored the castle, which had become somewhat dilapidated, and strengthened it to prepare for the threat of the Armada. In 1635 it passed to the Attorney-General, Sir John Bankes, who later became Chief Justice of the Common Pleas, spending most of his time with the king. In his absence it fell to Lady Bankes to defend this last Royalist stronghold in the south against Parliamentary forces. For almost three years she valiantly held out against the besiegers, but in 1646 treachery forced the inevitable surrender. The Parliamentarian forces plundered the castle of its riches before sacking it with a ferocity quite disproportionate to its importance.

In Corfe Village on the A351 Wareham to Swanage road, Dorset, England (OS reference SY958823). Tel: 01929 481294

Points of Interest
1. Outer bridge and gatehouse
2. South-west gatehouse (Edward the Martyr's Gate)
3. South tower or Gaoler's Tower
4. Butavant or Dungeon Tower
5. North tower (prison chapel)
6. Keep (King's Tower)
7. Gloriette apartments, including the King's Hall
8. Plukenet Tower
9. Horseshoe Tower

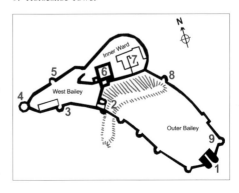

Dunstanburgh Castle

The Earl of Lancaster's Gatehouse

There can be few more dramatic and spectacularly lonely sights than that of Dunstanburgh Castle on the wild Northumberland coast. Perched on a rocky headland jutting out into the North Sea, it is surrounded on three sides by the precipices of Gull Crag and Saddle Rock, and Rumble Churn, an aptly named ravine lashed by the ferocious water. Throughout the forty-five-minute walk from the pretty fishing village of Craster along the headland, the rocky beach on the right, the castle stays within sight and one's strides lengthen in anticipation. The gaunt and skeletal shape of the gatehouse guides the wanderer unerringly to the castle entrance. When first built, the three-storey structure with its massive projecting curved drum towers must have appeared quite intimidating to anyone with nefarious intent, and in its crumbling state it still impresses. So does the sheer extent of the enclosure wall interspersed with broken towers and enclosing an area of some 4.5 hectares (11 acres).

The defensive strength of its walls, its carefully chosen location and the fury of the sea combined to frighten the marauding Scots against whom Thomas, Earl of Lancaster, the most powerful and wealthiest man in the land, began to build Dunstanburgh in 1313. But this was not the only reason. As instigator of the murder of Edward II's homosexual lover, Piers Gaveston, in summer 1312, Thomas found himself in need of protection against the king's wrath, and this remote corner of the realm seemed ideal. Thomas was eventually pardoned and given command of the king's forces in the north, but continued to ferment dissent among the rebellious barons, for which he was executed for treason in 1322. By that time, the castle had been completed on a grand scale, with an immense enclosure sufficient to serve as a place of refuge for the earl and his tenants in times of danger, and a formidable gatehouse on which no expense was spared. Although now much ruined, the fine ashlar stone used in its construction recalls the desire of Thomas to match the splendour of the king's castles. A great deal of the three floors can still be seen, although nothing is left of the smaller top floor that supported a parapet walk across the entrance. The two D-shaped projecting towers continued up for another two floors. A climb up the spiral stair offers a birds-eye view.

John of Gaunt, third son of Edward III, who became Duke of Lancaster through marriage in 1361, rearranged the castle by building a second gatehouse to the north-west, which together with an enclosed inner ward provided a more conventional layout. The original gatehouse then served as the keep. Unfortunately, only the foundations survive of John of Gaunt's work, which began in 1383. In better shape is the early fourteenth century rectangular Lilburn Tower, so named after John de Lilleburn, who became keeper of the castle after Thomas' execution. The 18m (60ft) high turreted tower served principally as a watch tower and residence. Other substantial remains in the south curtain are the Constable's Tower, which has the remains of two fireplaces and a fine south-facing window with double lights and a window seat, and the Egyncleugh Tower, the suffix 'cleugh' meaning ravine. Egyncleugh Tower is aptly named as it commands the chasm below its east wall. It served as the water gate, which gave access to the inlet that permitted small supply boats to reach the castle at high tide.

While the Scots are known to have made frequent incursions in the surrounding areas, they never attacked the castle, which later came into the hands of the Crown when John of Gaunt's son usurped the throne as Henry IV. However, in 1462 during the Wars of the Roses, it was besieged by the Yorkists, who forced its commander, Sir Ralph Percy, to surrender or starve two years later. The castle suffered some destruction and although repairs were carried out intermittently, a survey of 1538 described it as 'a very ruinous house and of small strength'. It consequently played no part in the civil wars in the seventeenth century. If, while walking back to Craster in the twilight hours, you see a ghostly figure pacing the rocky headland below the castle, it is likely to be that of Sir Guy the Seeker on his endless quest to find a lost princess. Who the beautiful princess was has not been recorded, but it is believed to be John of Gaunt's first wife Blanche, who died of the plague in 1369.

Near Craster village, 14.5km (9m) NE of Alnwick, Northumberland, England (OS reference NU 258220). Tel: 01665 576231

The castle dominating the headland

The remains of fireplaces in the gatehouse

Points of interest
1. Earl of Lancaster's gatehouse
2. Foundations of John of Gaunt's gatehouse with flanking walls
3. Low wall surrounding the inner ward with a well and fragments of an oven
4. Lilburn Tower with the postern gate
5. Constable's Tower with the remains of a domestic building behind
6. Small south curtain turret
7. Egyncleugh Tower guarding the ravine below

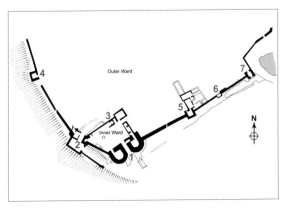

Etal Castle

This small border castle was built by the Manners family, which, under Robert Manners, is believed to have held the manor of Etal within the barony of Woolmer as early as 1180. It is likely that the early dwelling consisted of a simple timber manor within a palisaded enclosure. A stone tower house replaced the timber buildings some time in the late thirteenth or early fourteenth century, but it was when Edward III initiated his campaign to finally subjugate the Scots that local landowners began fortifying their houses as protection against the increasingly devastating raids over the English border. Thus, in 1341, Robert Manners obtained a licence to fortify his house by adding another level and crenellations to the three-storey structure. According to later surveys of the border fortifications, Etal was transformed from a fortalice, a building short of a castle, into a full castle, suggesting that Robert's son John had added the curtain wall, towers and gatehouse by 1368. The castle's subsequent history was marked by a lengthy and bitter dispute with the neighbouring Herons of Ford, but took on national importance in 1513, when James IV invaded England and captured and garrisoned Etal before his decisive defeat at the Battle of Flodden. The Manners family had by then already vacated the castle, and although it continued to be occupied by a constable, a lack of repairs led to gradual decay.

The rectangular keep

While the Castle is still a dominant presence in the picturesque village of the same name, the ruined tower house, gatehouse and south-west tower connected by a stretch of curtain wall are all that remains of this relatively modest border stronghold. The rectangular tower stands to almost full height, although the crenellations have gone, and only remnants have survived of the projecting forebuilding, which housed the main portcullised entrance and the spiral staircase that led to the upper storeys. The principal room was on the first floor, as marked by the remains of double windows with window seats and a wide arched fireplace. Notable in the two-storey gatehouse, now without its turreted flanking towers, are the guardroom, remains of the chapel and a fine traceried window above the slots for the cables of the portcullis and drawbridge. The ground floor chamber of the south-west tower is roofed by a stone vault, but there is little left of the upper level. Two corbels on the south wall once supported an overhanging latrine.

In Etal village, on B6354, 16km (10 miles) SW of Berwick-on-Tweed, Northumberland, England (OS reference NT 925394). Tel: 01890 820332.

The gatehouse

Eynsford Castle

The castle approach

A narrow alley off the main street of the pretty Kent village of the same name leads to this small castle, erected on an earth platform raised in Saxon times in the flood plain of the River Darent, which flows past Eynsford to the north-west. The Saxon fortification was protected by a ditch, which was later used to create the now dry moat. Although little known, Eynsford Castle is one of the earliest Norman stonework defences in the country, having been built in about 1088, when the earlier wooden tower was enclosed by a 6m (20ft) high and 1.8m (6ft) thick curtain wall of flint rubble laid in courses. A close examination of the wall reveals different materials and workmanship, mainly in the use of Roman tiles for dressing, suggesting two stages of construction with the second, an increase in height to some 9.1m (30ft) dating from around 1100. The building of the castle is credited to William de Eynsford I (FitzRalf), whose ancestors were either Danish or Norman, and who was given the lordship of Eynsford by Lanfranc, Archbishop of Canterbury. It remained in the hands of seven successive lords of the manor, but its occupation was relatively brief. A dispute over inheritance led to the raiding and sacking of the castle by two wronged families in 1312, which made it uninhabitable and ruinous.

Most of the enclosure wall remains standing, but only the foundations are left of the stone gate tower. Nothing at all has survived of the original wooden bridge with a drawbridge section at the castle end, although parts of the stone piers for a later bridge are still visible. The largest structure inside is the hall, which unfortunately extends little above the undercroft, having been gutted by fire in the early 1200s. Three arches, of which only the two pillars remain, would have supported the floor of the hall.

The smaller undercroft under the solar was a self-contained apartment with a fireplace and had its own entrance. As with the hall, nothing is left of the solar above. A forebuilding to the hall and a new kitchen were added later. A large framed opening in the north wall was a garderobe, reached by a wooden bridge from the hall. Three other large openings in the south-west corner indicate the presence of more garderobes, which discharged into the moat below. Other points of interest are the original great kitchen in the north-west corner and adjacent well.

In Eynsford village off A225 between Dartford and Sevenoaks, Kent, England (OS reference TQ 542658). Unattended

The fireplace in the solar undercroft

Farleigh Hungerford Castle

The romantic setting of the ruins of Farleigh Hungerford Castle in the green valley of the River Frome in Somerset belies a colourful and sometimes tragic past. Originally built as a manor house by the Montfort family and known as Farleigh Montfort, it passed in 1369 into the hands of Sir Thomas Hungerford, 'citizen and merchant of New Sarum'. Sir Thomas was steward to John of Gaunt and became the first recorded Speaker of the House of Commons in 1377. He proceeded to fortify the manor house with a quadrangular curtain wall and cylindrical towers at the corners, not so much for defensive purposes but as a sign of power and wealth. He did so without a royal licence, but is believed to have been granted a pardon in 1383. Sir Thomas died in 1398 and lies buried with his wife in St Anne's chapel at the castle.

A coat of arms over the gatehouse

Farleigh Montfort passed to his son Sir Walter Hungerford, who was a distinguished soldier and comrade of Henry V at Agincourt, and also followed his father into the Commons as Speaker before taking his seat in the House of Lords as Baron Hungerford. It was then that the castle was enlarged with an outer court surrounded by a curtain wall and renamed. He rose to be Lord High Treasurer, but the standing of the family suffered after his death in 1449. Robert, the 3rd baron, better known as Lord Moleyns, was executed in 1464 after the battle at Hexham, as was his son, Thomas, five years later. Farleigh passed into other hands in 1462, but was recovered by his youngest son, Sir Walter, in 1486. Lady Agnes, the second wife of his only heir, Sir Edward, was hanged at Tyburn in 1523 with her accomplice after being found guilty of strangling her first husband John Cotell and burning him in the kitchen furnace. Her ghost has been seen near the crypt.

Sir Edward's son, Walter, who became Lord Hungerford of Heytesbury in 1536, was by all accounts an unpleasant man. In a letter to Thomas Cromwell, his third wife complained of being imprisoned in a tower for four years with little food and drink, and of attempts to poison her. But Lord Hungerford himself was executed in 1540 for treason and 'unnatural vice', and Farleigh again passed to the king, although Queen Mary sold it back to his elder son, Sir Walter, later known as 'the Knight of Farley', in 1554. Sir Walter charged his second wife with adultery and attempted poisoning, but the case was dismissed and he finished up in prison when he refused to pay her costs. During the Civil War, members of the Hungerford family took different sides, and Sir Edward from the Black Burton strand of the family occupied the castle. Known as 'the Spendthrift' or 'Hungerford the Waster', he gambled away twenty-eight manors and eventually sold the castle in 1686, after which it fell into disrepair.

The Chapel and south-east tower

Lead coffins in the crypt

Much of the curtain walls, two of the flanking towers, and an imposing gatehouse with the arms richly carved in stone, remain to attest to the power once held by the Hungerfords, who rose to high office and entertained King Charles II about 1675, but ended in ignominy. But Farleigh Hungerford continues to impress the visitor today as it did London antiquary John Leland in the sixteenth century, who on his tour of Somerset noted that it 'was strong, set on a steep hill, with a stream in a ravine covering its rear' and had 'diverse pretty towers'. The inner buildings have virtually perished, save the outline of the foundations and the ancient adjoining chapels of St Anne and St Leonard, which remain surprisingly intact. The chapels are adorned with medieval wall paintings and house memorial tombs to some of the Hungerfords, including Sir Thomas and Sir Edward and their wives. In the crypt is an important collection of lead coffins dating from the sixteenth and seventeenth centuries.

Farleigh Hungerford on A366, 5.5km (3.5 miles) W of Trowbridge, Somerset, England (OS reference ST 801577). Tel: 01225 754026

Points of Interest
1. Two-storey east gate with sickle badge and family coat of arms
2. South-west (Lady) tower
3. Foundations of domestic buildings with the infamous kitchen furnace
4. South-east tower
5. Chapels of St Leonard and St Anne with medieval wall paintings and memorial tombs
6. Crypt with an important collection of lead coffins
7. The Priest's House

The south-west or Lady Tower

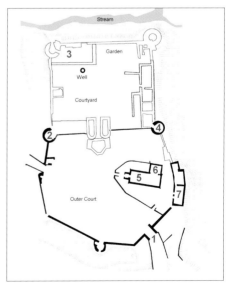

Framlingham Castle

The castle from across the mere

Once a hotbed of baronial conspiracy against the Crown, this remarkably early example of a 'keepless' castle today reposes majestically atop man made earthworks, lifting it out of the generally flat Suffolk countryside. Its soaring Norman curtain wall, studded with thirteen rectangular flanking towers reflected in the still waters of the Mere below the lower court, produces a most picturesque and memorable view. The towers are topped with tall ornamented brick-built chimneys, which serve as a reminder of its later days as a Tudor mansion. From the outside, Framlingham Castle has changed little in its 800-year history, but nothing remains of the original buildings within the walls, with the exception of a poorhouse built long after the castle had fallen into ruin. This lack of reminders of life inside the castle is more than made up for by the walk around the high battlements, which affords exceptional views and provides a superb perspective of Framlingham's defences. Each tower had a fighting gallery at its turreted top and was built with an open back. The resultant gap in the wall-walk was bridged with wooden gangways, which could be removed to stop attackers who had succeeded in reaching the battlements from fighting their way around the wall and controlling the interior.

The history of the castle shows how necessary this protection was, at least during the early time of the treacherous Bigods, who schemed and plotted against various kings for control of East Anglia. But a fortification existed at Framlingham long before the Normans arrived and King Edmund is thought to have sought protection there after a battle with the Danes, before being murdered in the nearby forests in

870. The manor of Framlingham was given by Henry I to Roger Bigod in 1101 and later passed to his second son Hugh, who proceeded with his fellow barons to take up arms against reigning monarchs, often changing sides when it suited his interests. After being created Earl of Norfolk in 1140, he built a wooden castle at Framlingham, but this was dismantled in 1173 on the orders of Henry II after the earl had backed a rebellion by Henry's eldest son. Hugh's son, another Roger, constructed the stone castle of today after Henry's death in 1189 and the succession to the throne of Richard the Lionheart.

When John became king ten years later, Roger gained favour, but he sided with the barons in the movement which resulted in the Magna Carta in 1215, and the king attacked Framlingham Castle the next year, forcing a surrender after just two days. Under Henry III, Framlingham was restored to Roger and subsequent earls remained loyal to the king until Roger Bigod IV, the 5th Earl of Norfolk, opposed Edward I's call for an invasion of France in 1297 and refused to go to Gascony while the king went to Flanders. 'Without you, O King, I am not bound to go, and go I will not,' Roger said to the king, who replied 'By God, sir Earl, you shall either go or hang.' Roger countered by saying 'By God, O King, I shall neither go nor hang.' And he did not, but it was the last hurrah of the Bigod earls of Norfolk. After Roger's death in 1307, the title and estates went to the Crown, which administered Framlingham until Thomas Mowbray was made Duke of Norfolk by Richard II in 1397.

Framlingham came into the possession of the Howards through Ann Mowbray, who was engaged

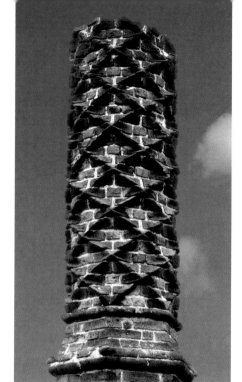

A decorative Tudor chimney

Off B1116 N of Framlingham town centre, Suffolk, England (OS reference TM 287637). Tel: 01728 724189

Points of Interest
1. Main gate surmounted by the Howard coat of arms
2. Wall-walk covering all thirteen towers, most fitted with Tudor chimneys
3. Site of the first hall and chapel with two chimney stacks and traces of Norman fireplaces
4. Poorhouse with the remains of a Norman hall and medieval crowned stone heads above the entrance
5. Projecting prison tower guarding the lower court
6. Gateway to the lower court with aspiral staircase
7. Stone piers, which once supported a bridge across the castle ditch leading to a deer park beyond

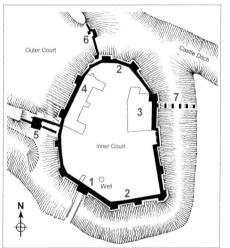

to Richard, Duke of York, one of the two princes executed in the Tower of London. John Howard led the royal army at the battle of Bosworth, but his son Thomas crossed Henry VIII. He was saved from execution be Henry's sudden death in 1547. Henry's son Edward VI gave Framlingham to his sister Mary Tudor in 1553, and it was there during that summer that Mary awaited news of her succession, before moving to London to oust Lady Jane Grey as Queen of England. The castle later passed back and forth between the Crown and the Howards, who finally sold it in 1635 to Sir Robert Hitcham.

Open towers in the east curtain wall

Goodrich Castle

This sturdy, pale red sandstone castle stands on a rocky summit high above the picturesque Wye valley, with spectacular views across Herefordshire and towards the eyrie of Symonds Yat. There can be few more majestically sited castles anywhere, with the added bonus that its walls are remarkably well preserved, in spite of slighting ordered by Parliament after the Civil War. The steep slope offered natural protection and there are signs that this lofty crag may already have been occupied in prehistoric times. When the Norman castle was built, its more vulnerable side was additionally guarded by a moat cut out of the rock, creating a strongly defendable fortification while also providing a comfortable and impressive baronial residence. The approach to the castle leads through a semi-circular barbican, which is connected to the outer enclosure wall that covers the north and east and provided the first line of defence. A sloping causeway and bridge connects the barbican to the ruinous north-east Tower, which served as a gatehouse. A 15m (50ft) vaulted corridor was barred at each end by a portcullis operated from an upstairs room. The upper floor in the tower also housed an apsidal chapel, recognisable from the outside by the decorated three-light window, now blocked up.

The oldest standing remains within the castle walls are the small 7.6m × 7.6m (25ft × 25ft) square

The portcullis slot

tower keep built in about 1160–70, probably upon the site of an earlier wooden castle of which nothing has been found. The walls of the keep were protected by clasping pillar buttresses all the way up at the corners and some two-thirds height at mid-wall. The three-storey tower has lost some of its height, including its battlements, but still reaches 18.3m (60ft) today. The first-floor entrance with a round-headed arch was probably reached by a wooden stair, as there is no evidence of a forebuilding. A spiral staircase in the north-west angle gave access to the upper floors. An arched doorway with chevron decoration was later added at basement level when the castle's usefulness as a fortress had ended. Of note are two original windows and chevron string coursing near the top of the keep.

For a hundred years, the keep stood alone, but William de Valence, who was created Earl of Pembroke in 1251, converted the castle into an impressive residence, without neglecting the need for a strong defensive capability. Earl William surrounded the keep with a quadrangular enclosure with massive cylindrical towers on three corners and the gatehouse tower, thus creating an inner ward. The cylindrical towers were provided with extending spurs that firmly clamped them to the bedrock base on which they were erected. Within the enclosure stood an

The curtain wall and towers built into the solid rock, with the keep behind

The barbican approach to the gatehouse

impressive great hall, measuring 20m × 8.2m (65ft × 27ft), an adjacent solar and small chapel for the use of the lord and his family, and the kitchens. There are the remains of several buildings also on the east range, although their purpose is unclear, as is the early history of the castle.

It is thought that the first owner was the English *Thegn* Godric, the then wooden fortress being known as Godric's Castle in the early twelfth century. The FitzBaderons, a minor noble family, may then have lived there, before it came into the ownership of the powerful Gilbert de Clare, who was created Earl of Pembroke in 1138. Another earl, William Marshall, said to have been 'the best knight in Christendom', defeated besieging barons beneath its walls in 1216. William's five sons were all lords of the castle and died in tragic circumstances, the fourth, Walter, at

Goodrich in 1245. The curse of a wronged Welsh prince was said to have caused their deaths. After the ownership of de Valence, Goodrich Castle became the principal residence through marriage of the Talbot family, who in 1442 were given the earldom of Shrewsbury. The castle was held briefly for Parliament early in the Civil War, before becoming a royal stronghold. But Cromwell did not give up and the garrison was forced to surrender in 1646, when the Parliamentarians laid siege and threatened to undermine and blow up its walls. It was partially demolished and allowed to fall into ruin.

In Goodrich village off A40, 8km (5 miles) S of Ross-on-Wye, Hereford & Worcester, England (OS reference SO 579199). Tel: 01600 890538

Points of interest
1. Entrance gate and semicircular barbican
2. North-east gatehouse tower with vaulted passage
3. Chapel tower
4. South-east tower
5. Great tower keep
6. South-west tower containing traces of foundations of an earlier tower
7. Remains of the great hall
8. North-west tower
9. East range

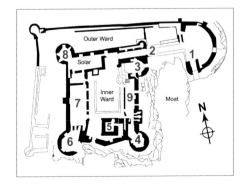

The solar and north-west tower

45

Hadleigh Castle

The south-east tower overlooking the Thames Estuary

A gentle climb along the hillside sloping up from a gully brings the visitor to the entrance of a much-ruined castle that stands defiantly on a narrow, windy ridge overlooking the Essex Marshes. In the distance, the wide expanse of the Thames Estuary provides some light relief to the bleak landscape, which is also surrounded by the urban and industrial sprawls of Canvey Island and South Benfleet. Neither Hadleigh Castle's sparse remains nor its less than romantic setting should be allowed to overshadow its historic interest. It has also been immortalised by one of the great landscape painters, John Constable, for whom it became a favourite subject. The dominant subject in Constable's studies is the south-east tower, one of three round towers built of rubble with ashlar dressings and the only one standing to nearly full height, although only the outer shell survives. The north-east tower, although still sizeable, lost much of its shape when it partially collapsed as a result of considerable landslip activity that encroached on the castle both from north and south. Landslip also caused the undermining and break-up of the south curtain wall and the disappearance of the King's Chamber and chapel. Still discernible is the barbican that protected the entrance and the adjacent High Tower. Outlines of the hall, domestic quarters and kitchen remain in the form of raised foundations.

A smelting furnace

The Castle was built by Hubert de Burgh, Justiciar of England and Earl of Kent, at the time of King John and the young Henry III. He received a licence to crenellate in 1230 and began work the following year with Kentish stone ferried across the river and to the castle by a now silted up creek. At the time, Hugh de Burgh was one of the most influential barons, but fell from royal favour in 1232, although work was allowed to continue. Edward III, concerned about a possible French attempt to move on London, spent considerable sums between 1361 and 1370 on strengthening the polygonal enclosure with several drum towers and a barbican, while also adding a great hall, chapel and royal suites. However, the castle's defences were never put to the test. For nearly 200 years it was granted 'for life' to a succession of queens, among them three of Henry VIII's wives, Catherine of Aragon, Catherine Parr and the 'Flanders Mare', Anne of Cleves, who lived at Hadleigh for a time after her divorce. In 1551, Edward VI sold it to Lord Riche, who allowed its stone to be used in other buildings.

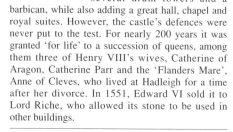

At Hadleigh village S of A13, 8km (5 miles) W of Southend-on-Sea, Essex, England (OS reference TQ 810860). Tel: 01760 755161

Hedingham Castle

A dense ring of mature trees where once stood an encircling curtain wall cannot hide the massive Norman keep of Hedingham which thrusts its almost perfect shape into the Essex sky. Towering above the town that grew up around its base, it remains an enduring monument to the great de Vere earls of Oxford. Aubrey 'Albericus' de Ver, who probably hailed from the small town of Ver in Normandy, obtained vast estates from William the Conqueror in 1066, stretching from East Anglia all the way down to what is now London. But it was his eldest son, Aubrey II, who started erecting the great stone keep in 1140, employing as his architect William de Corbeuil, Archbishop of Canterbury, who had previously designed the huge keep at Rochester. Rectangular in plan and measuring some 18.9m × 16.8m (62ft × 55ft), the keep features a splayed plinth with flat pilaster buttresses on the angles and mid-wall, and today stands 27.4m (90ft) tall, with two corner turrets extending another 6m (20ft). Its walls are up to 4m (13ft) thick and are faced with expensive ashlar stone from the quarries at Barnack in Northamptonshire.

A Norman stone arch in the great hall

The earls were fighting men of great valour, and were mostly loyal to their king. There were, however, a few exceptions. Robert, the 3rd Earl, took up arms against King John, and with other barons, compelled him to accede to the Magna Carta. King John resisted subsequent moves to replace him with Prince Louis of France and laid siege to Hedingham Castle in 1216, forcing a surrender, albeit only after fierce resistance. It was retaken by Prince Louis the following year.

The impressive keep is approached via a beautiful Tudor bridge, built around 1496 to replace the drawbridge, which spans the dry moat and leads to the inner bailey. The forebuilding is now no more, with only the overgrown dungeon visible from the first-floor entrance to the keep. The rounded arch over the main door still has its typical chevroned Norman decoration, a theme which, with variations, has been repeated inside. A small passage opens out into the magnificent two-storey banqueting or great hall with finely carved stonework and a spectacular stone arch, said to be the largest Norman arch in Europe. The best view can be had from the minstrel gallery above, which runs all the way round and is built within the thickness of the walls. Henry VII, Henry VIII and Queen Elizabeth I were all lavishly entertained at Hedingham.

Off A604 above town of Castle Hedingham, Essex, England (OS reference TL 787359). Tel: 01787 460261. Web: www.hedinghamcastle.co.uk

The tower keep

Helmsley Castle

Sited on a modest rocky outcrop overlooking the river Rye and the town of Helmsley, this castle was built around 1120 by Walter l'Espec, Lord of Helmsley, marking the centre of his vast estates in North Yorkshire. It is remarkable for its massive rectangular earthworks which once protected a timber fortification, and, although now softened by a covering of grass and blending in with the surrounding green pastures, the deep ditches still appear formidable obstacles to any would-be assailant. No traces can be found of the original timber buildings, but the surviving stone structures provide evidence of several building periods, starting with the first stone castle erected by Robert de Roos between 1186 and 1227. The de Rooses had succeeded to the lordship of Helmsley after the death of l'Espec in 1154 through the marriage of his sister Adeline to Peter de Roos. Walter l'Espec had no heir, his only son having been killed in a riding accident in the area around Kirkham, which prompted him to found a priory, believed to be near the spot where his son died. The cartulary of Rievaulx Abbey, also founded by l'Espec, confirms that Robert 'raised the castles at Helmislay and Wark'.

Robert de Roos levelled off the inner bank and replaced it with a stone curtain wall, fortified with round towers at the corners, and added two entrances. The main entrance at the south-eastern corner was protected by a strong square tower, while another gatehouse, flanked by round towers, pierced the centre of the north curtain. Two great towers, one midway along the eastern wall and overlooking the town, and the other in the opposite western curtain wall, completed the extensive defences. In 1246, a new chapel was consecrated near the east tower, but little further building work was undertaken until Robert's grandson, also named Robert, added barbicans to strengthen the north and south gates.

The de Rooses considerably increased their estates through astute marriages, and Robert's son William, Lord Ros of Helmsley and Belvoir, continued to develop the castle to underscore the family's new wealth and standing. His major contribution was a splendid new hall, which abutted the west tower. The tower itself was converted into private apartments for the lord and his family. Other domestic buildings were added or upgraded. The lordship of Helmsley remained in the family until 1689, except for a short period from 1478, when Edmund de Roos sold it to Richard, Duke of Gloucester, later to become Richard III. It was restored in 1485 after Richard's death at the Battle of Bosworth, and when Edmund died without heir, the lordship passed to his cousin, Sir George Manners, the Earl of Rutland. It was his grandson, Edward, the 3rd Earl, who remodelled the west tower and hall

The west tower by the inner ditch

48   *The south barbican*

into a Tudor mansion. The castle never saw action until the Civil War, when, after a three-month siege in 1644, it was surrendered to the Parliamentarian forces and slighted.

The main entrance to the castle is through the south barbican gatehouse, which still stands to a good height, flanked by open-backed drum towers and connected by a short curtain wall on each side to rounded towers. A timber bridge has replaced the drawbridge over the massive inner ditch to the original castle gate, but the abutments can still be appreciated. The bridge led to the original castle gate, which is now much ruined, as are the stone curtain walls around the inner bailey. Although it was blown up during the Civil War, with its eastern round-fronted half ripped out, the east tower remains the dominant feature of the castle. None of the floors above the basement now survive, but the crenellations and angle turrets on the west face are well preserved. On the open side, the joint between the original height and the fourteenth-century extension is clearly marked. The shells of the west tower and mansion also survive, but only the foundations remain of the northern corner towers and gate.

Close to Helmsley town centre, North Yorkshire, England (OS reference SE 611836).
Tel: 01439 770442

Points of interest
1. South barbican and gatehouse with open-backed drum towers
2. Bridge over the inner ditch and the remains of the rectangular gate tower
3. East tower with surviving crenellations and angle turrets
4. Foundations of the north gate
5. Old hall and Tudor mansion
6. Shell of the west tower
7. South-western corner tower

The east tower

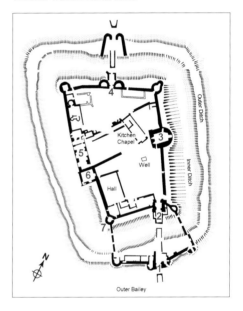

The old hall and mansion

49

Kenilworth Castle

The caste from the site of the Great Mere

In its prime, Kenilworth Castle was the most important lake-fortress in the realm, exceeding in size all others. The first castle was built on a sand and gravel spur between two brooks, possibly by Geoffrey de Clinton, chamberlain and treasurer to Henry I in about 1122, but more likely by Geoffrey II, after the death of his father in 1129. Henry II later leased it to have a stronghold close to Warwick, which was growing more powerful by the day, before it came permanently to the Crown. Succeeding monarchs, led by John and Henry III, spent vast sums of money to make it impregnable, the latter being credited with creating the 45ha (111 acre) artificial lake, closing all access routes to the castle, save along the narrow and well-defended crest of the dam. Neither attacks with a siege engine and artillery nor a water-borne assault could breach its defences when they were called upon in 1266. With the surrounding mere now long gone, having been drained in the seventeenth century to create pasture for cattle, it now requires a

A Norman slit window

little imagination to recall its former glory. But, as its broken walls and towers rise majestically from the surrounding landscape, England's largest castle ruin retains an aura of invincibility.

In 1254, Henry bequeathed the castle to his sister Eleanor, wife of Simon de Montfort, Earl of Leicester, little knowing that ten years later the earl would become his greatest enemy. De Montfort used Kenilworth as the base from which he directed the revolt against the king, but took one step too far when he imprisoned the princes Edward and Richard

at the castle. This led to a lengthy and in the end successful siege in 1266, when deprivation and disease forced the garrison to surrender. The castle was given to Edmund 'Crouchback', before coming back to the Crown once more on the accession to the throne of the Lancaster heir as Henry IV. In the fourteenth century, John of Gaunt, a prolific builder, added the magnificent banqueting hall and many other residential buildings, but maintained the castle's defences.

Few additions were made in the next two centuries until Henry VIII built a lodging block in Tudor style, of which nothing remains. In 1563, Kenilworth was bequeathed by Elizabeth I to Robert Dudley, later Earl of Leicester, the last great builder at the castle. Elizabeth herself spent many days at Kenilworth on several visits. One three-week stay in 1575 was particularly notable, being described vividly in Gascoigne's *Princely Pleasures at Kenilworth*. For nineteen days, the earl put on lavish, non-stop entertainment, including masques and pageants, such as had never before been seen in the realm. After his death in 1588 the castle was eventually sold to James I. But neither James, nor his son Prince Henry cared much for it, and Charles I leased it in 1626 to the Earl of Monmouth. It was ordered to be slighted at the time of the Civil War, which resulted in the destruction of the north side of the keep and much of the outer walls, although it had already been left to decay long before then.

Much of its fabric has survived to near full height,

The great hall with fine windows

appreciate, especially John of Gaunt's great hall with its oriel windows and huge fireplaces, and the nearby Leicester's Building, a Tudor palace built by Robert Dudley, Earl of Leicester. The inner enclosure sits at the western end of a large outer ward, which is surrounded by a curtain wall and several mural towers. Mortimer's Tower guarded the narrow approach to the castle along the crest of the dam, with a barbican the first line of defence at the other end of the dam.

On B4103 W of Kenilworth town centre, Warwickshire, England (OS reference SP 278723). Tel: 01926 852078.

Points of interest
1. Mortimer's Tower
2. Leicester's Building
3. John of Gaunt's great hall
4. Norman keep
5. Swan tower
6. Leicester's gatehouse with the arms of Robert Dudley
7. Lunn's Tower
8. Water tower

including the rectangular Norman keep, which forms the north-east angle of the inner ward. Measuring 17.7m × 26.5m (58ft × 87ft), it is about 24.4m (80ft) tall, with its corner turrets slightly higher. Robert Dudley spoiled the Norman structure somewhat when he replaced the original small windows with large lights, to provide accommodation suitable for Queen Elizabeth I. But there is much else to

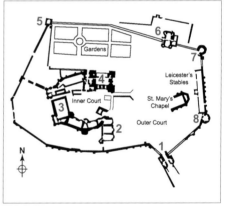

Leicester's Gatehouse

Kirby Muxloe Castle

Kirby Muxloe was one of three Leicestershire estates owned by William, Lord Hastings, Lord Chamberlain of England and a man of immense wealth. He was a prominent supporter of Edward IV, who in 1474 granted him a licence to fortify his manor houses and surround them with parkland. Building work at Kirby was started in autumn 1480, but Lord Hastings did not live to complete it, being summarily executed as a traitor by Richard III in June 1483. The picturesque ruin of this fortified manor house as seen today are much as Hastings left it; it was plundered for building stone after his death, and the work was never finished. But enough has survived of the structure and foundations to realise that it was on course to become one of the grandest manor houses in England. A complete record of the building works give a fascinating insight into the design and the vast sum of money spent on its ultimately incomplete construction. After Lord

The gatehouse

Hastings was beheaded, work continued on a reduced scale and stopped altogether at the end of 1484 after funds dried up.

The moated castle is approached over a bridge to the north-west gatehouse, which was defended by a drawbridge at the inner end, a portcullis and two sets of double doors, which prevented access through the four-centred entrance arch. There are four octagonal turrets at the corners, and other notable features are fragments of the Hastings arms on the right turret and embrasures and circular gunports in all four turrets, some of which are located below water level. The three-storey, 7.6m (25ft) square west tower is the best preserved, and was probably the only one of the four corner towers to be completed. It has square turrets on two sides, with an opening designed to lead out to the rampart walk. Little is left of the two-storey buildings that ranged from the gatehouse beyond fragments of walls and fireplaces, and other work, including the three middle towers, now stand no higher than a few brick courses above ground level. It is possible that this work was never finished. The construction throughout was in brick, with stone only being used for doorways and windows. Standing back from the road running through the village, this castle has surely lost none of its appeal. The reflection of its surviving red brick walls in the waters of the surrounding moat and its setting in lush parkland make for a very pretty sight.

In Kirby Muxloe village on minor road off B5380, 6km (4 miles) W of Leicester, Leicestershire, England (OS reference SK 524046). Tel: 01162 386886

The unfinished castle surrounded by its moat

Launceston Castle

The shell keep on the high motte

Rising from a large natural mound that dominates the market town of Launceston, the large shell keep enclosing a slimmer and taller central tower is virtually all that now remains of what once was a strong and strategically important castle. The only other surviving structures, albeit much ruined, are two gatehouses, one at the foot of the motte staircase, once fitted with two portcullises and a barbican, and the other protecting the southern bailey. The 12.2m (40ft) high, circular tower within the shell comprises two rooms, the upper featuring a large window with a seat and evidence of an impressive fireplace. The narrow gap between the tower and the outer shell was roofed over to provide a fighting platform for defence, as indicated by the corresponding beam-holes in the outer and inner circles. The wall at the foot of the motte, which separated the main defences from the bailey, has gone, and all other buildings within the castle were demolished when the grounds were landscaped. Other parts of the outer wards were over time incorporated into the town. Recent excavations have exposed remnants of the thirteenth century hall, which served as the County Assizes until the early 1600s.

The castle was raised soon after the Norman Conquest by Robert, Count of Mortain, half-brother to William I, who made Dunhevet, the medieval name for Launceston, the county town of Cornwall. It controlled the vast area between Bodmin Moor and Dartmoor, as well as the main river crossing point from Devon. Originally a motte-and-bailey with wooden defences, the circular stone keep was constructed in the late twelfth Century. But it was Richard of Cornwall, younger brother of Henry III, who transformed the castle between 1227 and 1272 by adding the curtain wall that skirted the original

The town gate

mound and great hall. He also rebuilt the gatehouse with formidable drum towers. Following the death of Richard in 1272, the administrative centre of Cornwall was moved to Lostwithiel and the castle declined and became ruinous. In 1337, Edward the Black Prince rode into Launceston Castle to be proclaimed the first Duke of Cornwall. After changing hands several times during the Civil War, Launceston was finally captured by the Parliamentarians in 1646 and slighted. The only habitable building thereafter was the north gate, which became an infamous prison.

In Launceston town centre, Cornwall, England (OS reference SX 330846). Tel: 01566 772365

53

Ludlow Castle

The castle from across the River Teme

The approach to Ludlow Castle entrance from the picturesque town is not the most inspiring, so it is advisable to cross the old stone bridge and view the castle first from the other side of the River Teme, which curls around its base. From that vantage point it stretches majestically along the steep ridge and it is easy to believe that it once was the most imposing and important castle in the Welsh Marches. In size and stature it has few equals and although its walls are now shattered and lifeless, it continues to dominate the rolling Shropshire countryside today, as it did when it served as the Council of the Marches of Wales in the fifteenth century. Within its walls were hatched some of the more dastardly plots in England's turbulent past, giving it an enduring place in history

Work on the castle began in around 1085 by Roger de Lacy, whose father, Walter de Lacy, had accompanied William the Conqueror during his invasion in 1066. Unlike most other early Norman castles, which comprised chiefly timber fortifications, Ludlow is thought to have been built in stone from the outset. Roger de Lacy's rebellion against William II and the later revolt of the barons against King Stephen proved a turbulent time for Ludlow, in which the disputes over ownership only added to its troubles. For a time, the castle was managed by Sir Joyce de Dinan, who is believed to have built the beautiful circular chapel in the inner ward and probably the outer ward. A great deal can be learned of life at the castle during that period from the *Geste of Fulk Fitzwarine*, a tale of an adventurous knight. Ludlow's illustrious reign began in 1306, when it passed by marriage to Roger Mortimer of nearby Wigmore Castle. The addition of the lordship of Ludlow made the Mortimers the most powerful family in the kingdom and Roger wasted no time in using his power. In 1326, in concert with

his lover Queen Isabella, he deposed Edward II and had him horrifically murdered at Berkeley Castle. During the minority of Edward III, Roger effectively ruled the country from his Ludlow stronghold, but the young king avenged the murder of his father by having Roger hanged at Tyburn in 1331.

The castle then came to the Crown, but was later returned to the Mortimers, who are credited with erecting the great buildings of the north front. Ludlow figured strongly during the bloody power struggle between the houses of Lancaster and York. In 1461, Edward, Duke of York, set out from the castle to defeat the Lancastrians at the battle of Mortimer's Cross and secured the throne for the House of York. After becoming Edward IV, he set up the Council of the Marches of Wales at Ludlow, leading to another period of expansion and wealth for town and castle. The princes Edward and Richard spent much time at the castle, but on their father's death in 1483, both were imprisoned by their uncle, Richard, Duke of Gloucester, later Richard III, in the Tower of London, where they were probably murdered. The most famous holder of the title Lord President of the Council was a favourite of Queen Elizabeth I, Sir Henry Sidney, who made extensive improvements and added the gatehouse in 1581. The castle was surrendered to the Parliamentarians in 1646, leading to a long period of neglect.

Much of the fabric of the castle has survived, making exploration of the inner ward a rewarding experience. The two jewels in the crown are the round chapel of St Mary Magdalene, the oldest of its type in Britain, which stands isolated in the middle of the ward and displays a beautifully preserved entrance with fine Norman chevron mouldings, and the five-storey buildings of the north front. Flanked by the Tower of Prince Arthur, older brother of Henry VIII, and the Tower of Pendover, which was

The decorated chapel doorway

Mortimer's Tower set into the western curtain wall of the outer ward.

Close to Ludlow town centre, Shropshire, England (OS reference SO 508746). Tel: 01584 873355

Points of interest
1. Mortimer's Tower
2. Stone bridge leading to the gatehouse
3. Rectangular keep
4. Small Norman tower with the remains of an oven
5. Prince Arthur's Tower
6. Great hall and state apartments
7. Princes' apartments in Pendover Tower
8. Round Norman chapel with fine decorations

occupied by the two tragic princes, are the remains of the state apartments and the impressive great hall, or council chamber. This is a magnificent high room measuring 18.3m × 9.15m (60ft × 30ft) and while it is now ruinous, it still easily recalls the splendour of times past. Access to the inner ward is by a stone bridge over the moat, which leads to the gatehouse and keep, built and remodelled by Sir Henry Sidney. Other fascinating features are the remains of the kitchen and a small Norman tower with an oven. The memory of Roger Mortimer has been kept alive by

The round Norman chapel

Middleham Castle

To some, the small Wensleydale town of Middleham is known for its horse racing, but for others who have had the pleasure of visiting its impressive castle, the figure of Richard, Duke of Gloucester, later Richard III, will forever be associated with this small town. In 1461, the young Richard was sent to Middleham, where for the next three years, he learned the arts of war and social graces under the tutelage of his cousin, Richard Neville, Earl of Warwick, often known as 'the Kingmaker'. After Warwick's death in 1471 at the Battle of Barnet, Richard received the lordships of Middleham, Sheriff Hutton and Penrith from his brother Edward IV, and the following year married Lady Anne Neville, through whom he acquired the lordship of Barnard. Middleham was his favourite castle and, as Lord of the North, he worked hard to bring peace to an often troublesome region. His only son Edward was born at the castle in 1474 and died there ten years later. Richard became king in 1483, but survived his son by only one year, being killed at the Battle of Bosworth in August 1485. After his death, Henry VII seized Middleham and the castle remained under the Crown until 1604.

Today's mighty ruin was not, however, the first castle to be built. This was a motte-and-bailey castle surrounded by a ditch, now known as William's Hill, a few hundred yards behind the current location. It was raised by Alan the Red, one of William the Conqueror's chief supporters, who was granted the land by Gilpatric. Alan's great grandson, Robert FitzRanulph is believed to have begun building the stone keep in about 1170–80, in the reign of Henry

II, in the centre of the present site, which was probably chosen more for comfort than any defensive qualities. No documentary evidence exists on the exact date, but a waterleaf carving in the small chapel is similar to the keep at Newcastle-upon-Tyne, which was built around the same period. A curtain wall enclosure surrounded by a wide ditch was erected during the thirteenth century, with the corner towers added around 1300. The Nevills inherited Middleham in 1270, when Robert de Nevill married Mary, daughter and heiress of Ralph FitzRanulph.

Empty and roofless though it may be, the imposing keep, one of the largest in England measuring 32m × 23.7m (105ft × 78ft) with walls 3.7m (12ft) thick, provides a powerful reminder of days long gone when it was the residence of some of the country's greatest lords. Although the entrance to the castle is now through the three-storey northern gate, in Richard's times it was through the east gate, of which only the foundations are now left. The keep naturally dominates the inner courtyard and was entered on the first level via a well-defended staircase. A round-headed doorway leads into the great hall, where the lord would have entertained and held court. Openings lead from the hall into a small chapel and the great chamber, which itself provided access to the lord's private apartment. Remnants of fireplaces can be found in both chambers. The kitchen, two wells and a cellar occupy the ground floor, reached by a spiral stair from the hall above. The remains of tracery windows suggest the presence of a large chapel on the upper

The view of the castle from above the town

The gatehouse and north-east tower

On edge of Middleham village off A6108, 3km (2 miles) S of Leyburn, North Yorkshire, England (OS reference SE 128875). Tel: 01969 623899

Points of interest
1. North gatehouse entrance
2. Remains of a three-storey building with upper chapel
3. Ovens and horse mill in the south range
4. Keep with kitchen and cellars on ground floor and great hall and chambers over
5. South-west or Prince's Tower
6. Bakehouse with nursery over
7. Garderobe tower
8. North-west tower

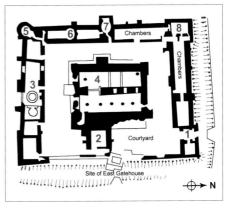

floor of a much-ruined three-storey building attached to the east wall of the keep.

The domestic buildings, all two storeys high, were built against the curtain wall and surrounded the keep on all four sides. The south range is notable for the remains of two ovens and a horse mill, while on the ground level of the south-east tower, a puzzling circular feature is thought to have been the base for a brewing vat. The south-west tower, or Prince's Tower, is generally believed to have been the birthplace of Richard's son Edward, that belief being based on a 1538 survey that talked of a nursee (nursery) right next to the tower. A modern bust of Richard III graces the inner courtyard.

The great hall

The remains of the chapel

57

Moreton Corbet Castle

The shell of the Elizabethan Mansion

In close proximity to Shawbury in rural Shropshire lies a most interesting historic site, comprising both a ruined Norman castle and a medieval hall, for long associated with the Corbet family. The broken walls span a 500-year period, beginning soon after the Norman Conquest, when a small fortified house, protected by a timber rampart and ditch, was constructed at Moreton Toret, as the site was then known. Bartholomew Toret is thought to have replaced the timber defences with a stone castle, starting building in about 1200, mainly as protection against lawless elements along the Welsh Marches. The keep was built first, with the gatehouse and curtain walls added some time later. The Torets were an old Saxon family who prospered under the Norman kings until Bartholomew was imprisoned by King John in 1215. The following year, Earl William Marshall of Pembroke took the castle after a short siege, but held it only briefly. It was renamed after it came into the ownership of the Corbet family, when Bartholomew's heiress Johanna married Richard Corbet in 1239. The Corbets hailed from Pays de Caux in Normandy and became an influential family in Shropshire.

The restored medieval gatehouse

One Corbet was involved in the death of Prince Llewelyn the Last of Wales in 1282, but the subsequent history of Morton Corbet proved relatively uneventful over the centuries until 1538 when Sir Andrew had the castle remodelled. The gatehouse was castellated and had a room in the sloping roof above the first-floor quarters. After Sir Andrew's death in 1579, which is commemorated by a plaque above the gatehouse arch, his son Robert, English Ambassador to Italy, embarked on the construction of a grand manor house. However, he died of the plague in 1583 and the house was never finished. The surviving façade of the Elizabethan wing in its majestically ruinous state, bare inside except for a large decorated fireplace, confirms the view of antiquarian William Camden who wrote that Robert 'with an affectionate delight of architecture began to build ... a most gorgeous and stately house after the Italian model'. During the Civil War, Sir Vincent fortified the castle in support of King Charles I and garrisoned it with a strong force of 110 men, who in summer 1644 repulsed two attacks by Parliamentarian forces. But the following September, ten troopers tricked the Royalists into surrender after a minor skirmish in the dead of the night. The castle was slighted and burned in 1645 and the Corbets never returned.

Off B5063, 11km (7 miles) NE of Shrewsbury, Shropshire, England (OS reference SJ 562232). Tel: 01604 730320

Set on a rise above the village on the south bank of the River Tweed, Norham Castle's ruins are dominated by the great keep, its bulky rectangular walls still reaching in part up to its full height of 27.4m (90ft). The site is protected on the north and east by a steep cliff rising from the river, a deep ravine on its eastern flank, and an artificially created deep hollow to the south, which leads into the river. The crescent-shaped outer ward and raised inner ward, both surrounded by a now much ruined curtain wall, were additionally guarded in parts by a moat and deep ditches. In spite of this natural defensive strength, Norham was repeatedly attacked and besieged during the thirteenth and fourteenth centuries, captured three times by the Scots, and finally stormed and largely destroyed by another Scot, James IV, in 1513, the defenders having no answer to an army equipped with guns. An extensive rebuilding programme was put in hand after the English victory at nearby Flodden Field. Bishop Ranulph Flambard of Durham constructed the first building on the site in 1121, but this lasted only fifteen years, before it was captured and held for a short time by David of Scotland in 1136. It was attacked again two years later, suffering considerable damage. Hugh de Puiset, Bishop of Durham, under orders from Henry II, rebuilt the castle on a grand scale between 1157 and 1170. Further sums were spent between 1208 and 1212 by King John, who is credited with building the Sheep Gate. King Edward I arbitrated at Norham between the thirteen competitors for the Scottish crown in 1291.

The surviving keep, originally three storeys tall, incorporates four building periods spanning four centuries, its stonework ranging from the twelfth century uneven ashlar walls to the regular horizontal string courses of the fifteenth century. Among the earliest parts are the groin-vaulted undercroft on the north side and the halls of bishops Flambard and Puiset on the first floor, and also of note is the base of the latrine added in 1429. In front of the keep are the remains of Clapham's Tower, built in 1515 for artillery. A gunport can still be seen in the basement. Other surviving elements of interest are Bishop Fox's aqueduct, which carried water into the moat, several low-level gun embrasures in the north curtain wall, the remains of the brewhouse in the bottom of the moat, the west gate, and the Sheep Gate, through which the castle is entered.

In Norham village on minor road off B6470, 12km (7.5 miles) SW of Berwick-on-Tweed, Northumberland, England (OS reference NT 907476). Tel: 01289 382329

The great tower from the west gate

The great tower in the inner ward

Nunney Castle

One may well ask what a medieval moated castle in the French style is doing tucked away in the middle of a sleepy Somerset village. It almost feels as if the castle is trying to hide among the pretty stone-walled cottages, and it is indeed little visited. But once discovered, it takes no more than a few minutes to complete the full circuit of this symmetrical castle, which is a simple rectangle with a large drum tower at each corner and machicolations at wall level all around. The waters of the moat come up to the foot of the walls. Curiously, the southern and northern towers are so close together that they almost touch. Although extensively damaged during the Civil War, sufficient remains to be impressive in its strength and grandeur. Crossing the moat via a wooden bridge, one goes straight into the castle through a plain doorway that had no portcullis. The hole in the wall to the right was caused by cannon fire. The floor area is surprisingly small, but there was accommodation on three floors, with a basement and extra floor in the towers. To stand in the centre of the keep, one can feel a keen sense of history all around – heightened by the silence. The only sound is the quacking of the ducks with their ducklings as they complete endless circuits of the deep moat.

The castle was built in 1393 by Sir John Delamere after he had obtained a licence to crenellate from Edward III. It is said that he financed the construction with ransom money obtained during his service in the French wars. Sir John, whose monument can be found in the nearby church, was clearly influenced by the French style of chateau, providing the castle with conical roofs on top of the four corner towers and a rampart wall-walk. The surviving corbels suggest that the walk was probably in timber and projected from the face of the castle. The interior arrangement comprised three storeys and a basement, accessed by a large staircase in the north-western tower. Still discernible are a hall with a large fireplace on the first floor, and a small chapel on the top level. Also of note are the mullioned windows of Early Perpendicular style. The beautiful ashlar masonry was neither strong nor thick enough to withstand cannon fire, and the loops were equally ineffective, being suitable only for bows and crossbows. When the Parliamentarians placed their cannon on rising ground overlooking the castle in 1645, the curtain wall was immediately breached above the entrance.

In Nunney village off A361, 5km (3 miles) SW of Frome, Somerset, England (OS reference ST 737457). Unattended

The great hall

The moated castle with its massive round towers

The lower bailey from the keep

Surrounded by lovely woodland in the valley of the River Okement and occupying a long and narrow shale outcrop on the northern edge of Dartmoor National Park, Okehampton Castle is dominated by the spectacularly jagged remains of the keep thrusting upwards into the sky. Compared to other castles in the realm, Okehampton is quite small, yet is the largest castle in the West Country. Although the surviving masonry dates mostly from the early 1300s and is the work of Earl Hugh Courtney, a member of a powerful local family, an earlier castle was established on this lofty spur probably around 1068 by Baldwin de Brionne, one of the knights of William the Conqueror. As Royal Sheriff of Devonshire, de Brionne originally raised a motte, protected by rock-cut ditches, before adding a stone keep before the end of the eleventh century. The castle served as an administrative centre for his large estates in Devon, but also had strong defences to guard the main route into Cornwall. Its history is extremely sketchy and frequent changes of ownership accompanied by occasional building work make it difficult to obtain a clear picture of its progress. This would suggest that life at the castle was relatively uneventful, with its defensive capabilities never put to the test. The only event of note came in 1539, when its owner, Henry, Marquis of Exeter, was found guilty of conspiracy and executed by Henry VIII. This led directly to the abandonment and subsequent neglect of Okehampton, although the presence of cobbled floors in parts of the castle would suggest some form of occupation into the seventeenth century.

The broken walls atop the imposing motte represent a remodelling of the original keep with thicker walls and rounded arched windows that let in

The castle approach from the town

more light and added to the comfort of the occupants. Other buildings along the ridge, many of which still stand to a good height, were also added around the same time, and include a kitchen, separated from the great hall by a cobbled screens passage, a solar, a guardroom and other domestic lodgings. The presence of a sedilia identifies the ruinous walls on the eastern side as those of a small chapel. Of particular interest is the cobbled Barbican Passage, a long narrow tunnel which provided restricted access from the northerly gatehouse to the entrance into the main enclosure. If the grass among the ruins appears increasingly sparse, it is possibly due to one of Devon's most famous ghosts, that of Lady Howard, who is said to make frequent visits from Tavistock to pluck a blade of grass as a penance for her sins. Only when she has finally 'mown' the castle site, will she be able to rest.

On minor road off B3260, 1km (½ mile) SW of Okehampton town centre, Devon, England (OS reference SX 584942). Tel: 01837 52844

Orford Castle

The keep, with its projecting square turrets

The majestic keep sitting atop massive earthworks is all that remains of what once was a formidable royal stronghold of that master castle builder Henry II. Today, as it did in its heyday, the keep towers above the small Suffolk village of Orford, and affords a commanding view over the river Alde and Orford Ness. The castle is remarkable in that the keep is polygonal on the outside, with three projecting turrets, and circular within – the only similar Norman keep is at Conisborough in South Yorkshire – and it incorporates a number of innovative features. The design provides for two self-contained floors, with the grander second almost certainly intended for Henry and his queen, Eleanor of Aquitaine. Orford is also unique in another respect. It is the earliest castle whose entire building records and accounts survive, which suggest that it was the most expensive castle to be built at that time. A total of £1,413 was spent on its construction, a staggering one-seventh of the King's estimated yearly income.

The reason Henry II spared no expense resided in nearby Framlingham Castle, where Hugh Bigod, Earl of Norfolk, who then controlled most of East Anglia, proved a constant threat to the king's authority. There was also the menace of a possible foreign invasion. Henry began building the keep in 1165, before surrounding it with a formidable curtain wall and towers, of which regrettably nothing remains. He also drained the marshes and turned the sleepy hamlet of Orford into a thriving port and market town. Immediately after completing the castle's construction in 1173 the king's rule faced its first challenge, when his eldest son rebelled, aided by Bigod and other treacherous barons, and supported by Flemish mercenaries. But Henry, who had the castle heavily reinforced with many men and much food, prevailed and ordered the destruction and confiscation of Bigod's citadel at Framlingham, thus gaining a measure of control over the troublesome region.

As a result, a relatively peaceful and uneventful period ensued, but in 1217 Louis, the French leader during fighting after the death of King John, captured Orford Castle. Nevertheless, it remained sufficiently important to be kept in reasonable repair throughout the thirteenth century. But its role as a centre of local government and symbol of royal authority, as well as its military usefulness, began to decline along with the port, as progressive silting up of the estuary caused trade to fall away. From 1280, in the reign of Edward I, it was granted out until in 1336, Edward III bequeathed it in perpetuity to Robert of Ufford who, a year later became Earl of Suffolk.

The lofty keep at Orford is in near perfect condition. The walls are a massive 3m (10ft) thick and are riddled with rooms and passages, most of which can be explored. The entrance is typically on the first level and the outer doorway has a low triangular arch similar to that at Framlingham. This gives access to a lobby, from which steep steps lead down to a cell. A splendid spiral staircase rises sheer from the basement to the top of the keep in an anti-clockwise direction, which made it difficult for an attacker climbing up to wield the sword in his right hand. The main entrance to the keep proper leads from the lobby to the lower circular hall. Surrounding the hall are two levels of passages including various rooms and apartments. Climbing up further, the stairway leads to the generally similar upper hall. Corbels high up in the wall once supported the original conical roof, while doorways open to guard chambers in the turrets. Again, there are a multitude of recesses and passages. The upper hall would have been lavishly appointed with decorative tiles, wall hangings and carved timbers thrusting high to support the original conical roof. Orford Castle was indeed a place fit for a king.

In Orford village off B1084, 11.5km (7 miles) E of Woodbridge, Suffolk, England (OS reference TM 419499). Tel: 01394 450472

Points of Interest
1. Outer entrance into the lobby with a low Norman triangular arch
2. Ornately carved capitals supporting the round arches over the entrance door to the lower hall
3. Lower circular hall with a stone bench all round, twin Norman windows and a large fireplace
4. Triangular chapel and chaplain's room in upper part of lower hall
5. Circular upper hall with passages leading to a kitchen, garderobes and private chambers
6. Turret with a well-preserved oven and baking chamber, partly floored with glazed tiles.
7. External latrine outfalls at the base of the wall

Latrine outfalls

Twin Norman windows

Pevensey Castle

By any measure, this castle, on high ground in the Sussex countryside not far from the sea, is an impressive sight. Entry is through the arched east gateway, and the enormous oval-shaped grassed outer bailey is surrounded by a virtually unbroken stretch of formidable curtain walling. It is quite a surprise to learn that the wall and the west gate, of which parts of the flanking towers remain, date from Roman times, incorporating only some additional strengthening ordered by William the Conqueror. But the focal point in one corner of this Roman enclosure is the partially moated medieval castle, which itself makes a powerful statement, having survived in a fair state. Taken together, the Pevensey Castle site represents one of Britain's oldest and most important strongholds, standing on what was once a peninsula surrounded by sea and salt marsh. Even after the castle fell out of use in Tudor times and became ruinous, its strategic position again came into play when a gun emplacement was constructed in the outer bailey against the threat of the Spanish Armada in 1588. Much more recently, a command and observation post was set up inside the castle and the perimeter fences were refortified, to guard against a possible invasion during the Second World War.

The original fort which served the town of Anderida has been dated to 290 AD and was one of nine Roman forts that defended the so-called Saxon Shore. The *Anglo-Saxon Chronicle* records that in 491 it was overrun by a Saxon raiding party and its inhabitants slaughtered. It came to prominence again in 1066 when William, Duke of Normandy sailed into the Bay of Pevensey and set up his campaign headquarters inside the Roman fort. After his victory at the Battle of Hastings, he granted it and the surrounding lands, known as the Rape of Pevensey,

to his half-brother Robert, Count of Mortain, who proceeded to strengthen its defences. These came in useful in 1088, when the Count backed the wrong son of the Conqueror and was besieged by William Rufus. Only starvation forced a truce between the warring factions. Building started on a large stone keep around 1100, with the strong enclosure wall and towers replacing the timber defences of the inner bailey in the mid-thirteenth century. Pevensey Castle changed hands frequently and was besieged several times, the last time in 1399, when in the absence of her husband in support of Henry Bolingbroke, Lady Joan Pelham successfully held out.

During the fifteenth century, the castle served as a state prison. Among the famous inmates were King James I of Scotland and Queen Joan of Navarre, second wife of Henry IV, who was accused by her stepson, Henry V, of plotting his death by witchcraft. By the mid-sixteenth century, it had fallen into ruin, but it remains a splendid example of medieval architecture. Surrounded on two sides by a moat, the curtain wall that separates the inner bailey from the Roman fort is punctuated by three massive towers and a gatehouse, and is virtually intact, except for its crenellated parapet. The wall was built by Peter de Savoy after he was granted the castle by Henry III in 1246. Only one of the D-shaped towers of the gatehouse, which flanked the vaulted entrance passage, is left standing. Below it was the prison, a deep and dank hole where the only access was via a trap door. Of note in the three great curtain towers is the unusual design, whereby each of the three floors had its own access. The basement was reached down a flight of steps leading from a porch built out from the inside of the tower, the ground floor along a short passage and the upper level through a doorway at wall-walk level.

The castle from the west

The north tower with the moat

Points of interest
1. Gatehouse with the flanking prison tower
2. North tower with the remains of springing that supported a vaulted basement
3. East tower
4. Foundations of the thirteenth-century chapel and castle well
5. Ruin of the rectangular keep with the bases of projecting towers
6. Postern Gate that gave access to medieval shore
7. South tower

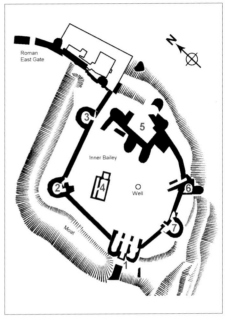

The outlines of the stone foundations of a chapel and the castle well can be seen set into the lawn of the inner bailey. The postern gate in the Roman wall that formed the eastern enclosure of the bailey once gave access to the shore. Alas, little of the great keep survives today; its most prominent features are the massive bases of two of the seven projecting towers, which gave the basically rectangular structure a strange appearance. Excavations have revealed the general outline, but dating accurately the various building periods and reconstructing the internal layout has so far eluded the experts.

In Pevensey village off A259, East Sussex, England (OS reference TQ 645048). Tel: 01323 762604

The inner ward with the remains of the chapel and the keep

The postern gate

Peveril Castle

This triangular 'Castle of the Peak' rises high above Castleton and it takes a little puff to negotiate the steep and winding path that leads up to the entrance. But at the end of the long climb, the visitor is repaid for the effort with breathtaking views. Situated on a high ridge, which slopes up sharply from the town to the south and is flanked by sheer drops into Cavedale on the other two sides, the castle was built to guard the valuable Peak Forest lead mines. It was built by one of William the Conqueror's most trusted knights, William Peveril, who was granted the title of Bailiff of the Royal Manors of the Peak and in 1080 erected a wooden keep. A stone curtain wall enclosure was added in 1090, one of the earliest to be constructed after the Norman Conquest. In 1114, his son, another William, inherited the castle and lands and probably built the chapel and hall. But he forfeited the estate in 1155 to Henry II after being implicated in the murder of the Earl of Chester. Henry rather liked this remote and inhospitable place, visiting it on many occasions to hunt. In 1157, King Malcolm of Scotland paid homage to the English king at the castle. Henry made many improvements and erected the tower keep in 1176. Henry III also visited it in the mid-thirteenth Century, when the new hall is assumed to have been built. Peveril Castle later changed hands several times until it became part of the vast Duchy of Lancaster when Edward III

The castle, with its prominent keep, from the town below

granted it to his son John of Gaunt. By then it had become obsolete and was partly dismantled. Its almost impregnable position ensured that its defences were never threatened.

The dominant feature is the simple 12.2m (40ft) square stone keep in the south-western corner, retaining most of its original height of 18.3m (60ft). Although small, the remains of the fine gritstone dressings on the more inaccessible side give an indication of its elegant appearance when first built. It had one main living room on the first floor, lit by windows on the inside walls only. Little can be recognised from the fragments of the original main gatehouse beside the keep, but what was the back gate and is now the entrance to the castle, remains in a much-ruined state. Large sections of the curtain wall stand, notable for its herringbone masonry, Roman tiles and small projecting turrets. It is possible to trace the foundations of the hall, chapel and kitchen within the courtyard.

On S side of Castleton off A6187, 24km (15 miles) W of Sheffield, England (OS reference SK150827). Tel: 01433 620613

Herringbone courses in the curtain wall

A few isolated copses interspersed in the wide expanse of fertile fields and moorland are all that remain of the extensive Forest of Pickering. Where once Edward II and successive monarchs accompanied by their noblemen rode out of the gatehouse of Pickering Castle to hunt game in the royal forest, there are now just the quiet comings and goings of visitors walking in their footsteps. Inside the castle, daily life in the later medieval period was more about entertaining than defending the realm, although its position on the edge of the North Yorkshire Moors and on the strategically important east–west route across the country, ensured that it was provided with highly capable defences. The large earth and stone mound that still dominates its surroundings at Pickering was the central feature of the first motte-and-bailey castle built by William the Conqueror in 1069. The timber castle was gradually replaced by stone fortifications, starting in 1180 when, according to surviving records, Henry II constructed the bridge to the inner ward, and probably added the enclosing curtain wall. The fortress was further strengthened under the reign of Henry III, who also built the chapel, which is still intact, and most likely the splendid hall of which only foundations remain. The outer stone curtain, towers and gatehouse were added under Edward II between 1323 and 1326. By the mid-sixteenth century, Pickering Castle was gradually falling into ruin and played no part in the Civil War.

The gatehouse entrance is approached over the deep ditch, which would have been spanned by a drawbridge, leading into the outer ward. The encircling curtain wall still stands mostly to wall-walk level, as do the three towers. The Diate Hill Tower to the right of the gatehouse was probably used by the captain of the guard. The northernmost Rosamund's Tower stands astride the inner ditch and has a small postern gate in the ditch bottom. The square Mill Tower with its circular turret at the south-western corner may have been named for the water mill that existed beside the Pickering Beck. The Coleman Tower, like all the others built in rubble and faced with ashlar, controlled the drawbridge and entrance to the inner ward. From here stone steps atop the wall spanning the inner ditch lead to the top of the motte and the remains of the shell keep, more commonly referred to as the King's Tower.

Short distance from Pickering town centre, 24km (15 miles) SW of Scarborough, North Yorkshire, England (OS reference SE 800845). Tel: 01751 474989

The view from the keep into the inner ward

Rosamund's Tower with the postern gate

The medieval castle within the Roman fort

This medieval 'hermit crab' castle occupies the north-west corner of a huge, almost perfect quadrangular, Roman fort that guarded against hostile approaches by sea. Much remains standing of the Norman enclosure, which is dominated by the great tower, which was built into the corner against the Roman wall, the tall structure being the first that comes into view when nearing the castle. But before entering, it is advisable first to circumnavigate the walls, which are surrounded by sea and ditches, to appreciate fully a history that stretches back some 1,700 years and to marvel at the skill of the Roman masons all those centuries ago, and the endurance of the walls and bastions. Once inside the enclosure, the sheer extent of the fort becomes clearer still, the Norman castle in the corner taking up but a small area. Also of interest is the church at the opposite end to the castle, which was built for an Augustinian priory in 1128 and survives with only the south transept missing. The priory was moved to nearby Southwick in 1147.

Portchester is a splendidly compact fortress and the near completeness of its buildings makes exploration easy and interesting. The inner enclosure walls were protected by a moat and drawbridge, which led to the gatehouse. This is a particularly compelling part of the castle. The original Norman gate projecting from the curtain wall was gradually extended outwards, first with a pair of semicircular walls, then with an inner gate and outer portcullis with a vaulted passage, which has survived virtually intact. The flanking walls were later lengthened again and another portcullis added to provide further protection to the drawbridge. The square great tower, faced with Caen ashlar stone and strengthened with pilaster buttresses at the corners and mid-wall, is in fine condition. It was originally built in about 1120 just two storeys high, but had a further two added before 1173. It is 17m (56ft) square and has walls 2.4m (8ft) thick. The forebuilding, which housed the chapel, also appears to have been rebuilt more than once. A wonderful view over Portchester harbour and across to the Isle of Wight can be had from the top of the tower.

Richard II's L-shaped palace, which occupies the western half of the inner bailey, stands almost complete except for its roof. The first floor comprised the public rooms, including a great hall and the great chamber, the principal state room. The hall was reached from a stair in the vaulted porch. The resplendent windows are now unfortunately without their ornate tracery. Other buildings of interest are the remains of the constable's house and Ashton's Tower, added by Sir Robert Ashton, who was constable in 1376–81.

The exact date of the building of the Norman stronghold is uncertain, but soon after the Conquest the Roman watergate, landgate and walls were refortified by William Mauduit, one of William I's supporters. After his son Robert was drowned, along with Henry I's son, in the *White Ship* disaster of 1120, the castle reverted to the Crown. Henry I made frequent use of the castle when sailing to Normandy, and it was also used to store treasury bullion. Henry II stayed at Portchester on several occasions, as did King John, who made modest additions, but he lost it in 1215 during the Barons' War, when the French captured it without resistance. In spite of occasional repairs, the buildings deteriorated over the next century and became ruinous. However, under

Richard II, a major rebuilding programme was initiated (1396–9), which included the addition of portcullises to all three gates, a more secure forebuilding to the tower, and the restructuring of the west range into a royal palace.

Edward II visited the castle a number of times, and Edward III stayed there in 1346 while assembling an army, which was later to become victorious at Crécy during the Hundred Years War with France. Henry V set out from Portchester in 1415 to his celebrated victory at Agincourt, but little of note transpired thereafter. The last castellan, Sir Thomas Cornwallis, apparently entertained Queen Elizabeth I at the castle in 1601. Portchester saw no action during the Civil War and escaped destruction, but was used as a prison during several subsequent wars.

On S side of Portchester off A27, Hampshire, England (OS reference SU 625046). Tel: 02393 378291

The entrance to Richard II's palace

The keep, showing the half-height buttresses

Points of interest
1. Roman Landgate remodelled in medieval times
2. Norman gatehouse with a vaulted passage
3. Richard II's palace with the great hall and great chamber
4. Great tower and ruined forebuilding with the remains of the chapel
5. Fragments of the constable's house
6. Ashton's Tower and the east range
7. Church with a decorated Norman west front

The water gate

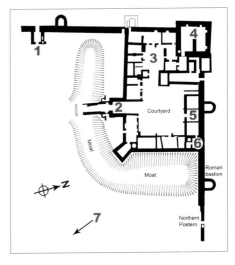

Prudhoe Castle

In spite of being set on the end of a steep-sided spur some 46m (150ft) above the River Tyne, Prudhoe Castle lies almost hidden behind a ring of dense, deciduous trees that shield the approach in summer. It comes into view only after crossing the dam between the millpond and the site of the mill and reaching the barbican, a spur of masonry designed to provide a first line of defence ahead of the gatehouse. Access to the outer ward is through rounded arches in the almost complete crenellated early twelfth century gatehouse, notable for its later chapel built into the upper storey. The chapel has narrow pointed lancet windows and an arch that leads into the sanctuary in the oriel window, considered one of the earliest to be found in any English castle. External stairs lead to the chapel and the battlements. The nineteenth century manor house was built against the remains of the tower keep, which was altered many times and is rather small when compared with other great keeps in the area. Originally only two storeys tall, it measured just 7.3m × 6.1m (24ft × 20ft) and had walls 3m (10ft) thick. Of interest are the stairs within the west wall of the keep. Of the drum towers that pierced the substantially complete curtain wall, only the shell of the north-west tower remains standing. Fragments of the service buildings, including the kitchens and brewhouse,

The barbican and gatehouse

have survived alongside the rectangular east tower.

A timber enclosure castle protected by massive ramparts and ditches was built by Robert d'Umfraville, who had been granted the barony of Prudhoe by Henry I. The first historical mention of the castle referred to two sieges by William the Lion, King of Scotland, in 1173 and 1174, both of which were resisted without much damage. However, Henry II agreed to the building of a stone castle to meet threats of further Scottish attacks. A square keep, one of the first in Northumberland, was constructed in 1175 and surrounded by a curtain wall and gatehouse. The castle entered a peaceful period until the Scottish Wars in the early fourteenth century when it was garrisoned, but it does not appear to have suffered further sieges. After coming into the possession of Henry Percy, Earl of Northumberland, through marriage in 1398, Prudhoe changed hands several times and gradually fell into decay after the execution of Sir Thomas Percy, who had joined the Pilgrimage of Grace in 1536.

N side of Prudhoe town on minor road off A695, 14km (8.75 miles) W of Newcastle-on-Tyne, Northumberland, England (OS reference NY 092634). Tel: 01661 833459

Restormel Castle

The crenellated shell keep

Perched on top of massive squat earthworks and surrounded by a now dry moat cut into the rock, Restormel Castle boasts an elegantly proportioned, almost circular shell keep, which at 38.1m (125ft) across is one of the largest in Britain. From the top of the wall-walk the view over the almost intact battlements across the rugged Cornish lands is quite magnificent. Any approaching enemy would have been spotted long before reaching the outer defences, but history shows that none tried to interrupt the idyllic and lavish lifestyle of its occupants. The stone keep replaced an earlier wooden one raised by the Norman knight Baldwin FitzTurstin around 1100, essentially to command the crossing point of the river Fowey. Within a few years, a square gateway tower with a drawbridge over the unusually wide and deep moat was added at the south-west, which remains the earliest stone structure on the site. The present stone keep dates from about 1200 and was built of dark local shillet, with door and window surrounds finished with high-quality cut stone, unfortunately pilfered after the castle's abandonment.

Restormel reached its zenith after Richard, second son of King John and brother of Henry III, became Earl of Cornwall in 1227 and moved the administrative centre from Launceston to nearby Lostwithiel. It was he and his son Edmund who are credited with adding the two-storey stone buildings against the inside of the shell, which provided accommodation for the guards and storage on the ground floor, and rather more splendid living quarters for the lord and lady on the upper level. The great hall is notable for its two large windows punched through the curtain wall and the door to the solar, which also has fine windows. More interesting still are the stairs from the solar that led to the wall-walk, which would have given the lord an excellent

The gatehouse with the bridge over the moat

view of the deer park that then surrounded the castle. There was also access from the solar to the chapel, which was added on the outside of the shell in 1280. Many of the inside walls have survived in good repair and although the floor has gone, the sockets for the floor beams can still be seen. A well was dug in the centre of the courtyard, but most of the water was brought into the castle by lead pipes from a nearby spring. Edward, the Black Prince, made it his home in the mid-fourteenth century, but after his death the castle fell into disrepair. It briefly saw action in the Civil War when it was captured from the Parliamentarians by Royalist Sir Richard Grenville in 1644.

On minor road off A390, 1.6km (1 mile) N of Lostwithiel, Cornwall, England (OS reference SX 104614). Tel: 01208 872687

Richmond Castle

The river view

Looking up from the banks of the river Swale, one sees the towering walls of Richmond Castle set spectacularly atop precipitous cliffs, forming the southern side of the huge triangular eminence known as Riche Mount on which the castle was built. On the other, still steep but more accessible, sides much thicker walls provided the necessary protection. No matter from which angle one approaches this immense ruined castle, it retains a commanding presence both over the valley of the river and over Richmond town. It is, therefore, no surprise to learn that it once was at the heart of one of the greatest estates in medieval England. Known later as the Honour of Richmond, it extended over eight counties and was a gift from William the Conqueror to his nephew Alan Rufus, Count of Penthièvre in Brittany, also known as Alan the Red. Although the origins of the castle are a little obscure, history scholars favour Count Alan as its builder, rather than William I himself.

What sets Richmond Castle apart from others in the realm, is the wealth of surviving eleventh century fabric, which makes it the best-preserved castle of its age. The enclosing curtain walling, the great gateway into the castle now embedded into the later keep, and Scolland's Hall, all date from Count Alan's time and were most likely constructed between 1070 and Alan's death in 1089. The most impressive early remains are those of Scolland's Hall, so named after a twelfth century constable of the castle. Set into the south-eastern corner, this rectangular two-storey building still stands to eaves level, with the line of square sockets that held the timber beams supporting the upper floor clearly

visible. The upper level contained a magnificent hall, which took up most of the floor space, and a solar at one end. Some of the original large twin windows survive intact on the southern side. The lower level was probably used for storage. Several alterations were made later, in part the result of an undocumented fire, which gutted the building around 1300. The east end of the hall was designed as a large gatehouse with the flanking Gold Hole Tower. Above the gate was a wooden gallery, from which the Count could admire the Cockpit Garden.

Most of the early curtain wall survives, as does one of the two towers along the eastern line of the enclosure. Known as Robin Hood's Tower, it contained two barrel-vaulted chambers, the lower of which was St Nicholas' chapel, notable for a central arch flanked by two roundels, which formed the backdrop to the high altar. An interesting feature when viewed from the outside is the projecting stonework around the altar window, which is intended to indicate the location of the chapel. Little remains of the other domestic buildings. The dominant feature of the castle is the great keep, which was built by Alan's son, Conan, Duke of Brittany, in the mid-twelfth century on top of the original gateway. A massive square structure with shallow buttresses and four corner turrets, the keep is 30.5m (100ft) high and comprises four floors, including a great hall on the upper level. The internal arrangement underwent major alterations under Henry III and Edward I, who spent considerable sums on Richmond. The basement vault and spiral stairs to the first floor are among the changes attributed to the latter.

When Duke Conan died in 1171, Richmond Castle passed for a time into royal hands, although the Dukes of Brittany continued to hold on to the Honour of Richmond for most of the next 300 years, until it was absorbed into the crown lands under Henry VII. The most noteworthy events during the preceding time were two confrontations between the castle's constable, Roald, and King John, and the opposition by the dukes to Henry III in 1265, but there are no records of Richmond having had to face a siege as a consequence. Its isolation ensured that it took no part in the Civil War, by which time it had already become ruinous.

Short distance from Richmond town centre, North Yorkshire, England (OS reference NZ 174006). Tel: 01748 822493

The inner gate to the keep

Points of interest
1. The great keep built over the eleventh century gateway
2. Robin Hood's Tower and St Nicholas' chapel
3. Scolland's Hall and the great chamber
4. Gold Hole Tower and the gatehouse
5. Cockpit Garden
6. North-west tower and postern gate

The great rectangular keep

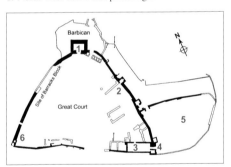

Scolland's Hall with the Gold Hole Tower

Rochester Castle

No matter from which direction one approaches the town, the massive Norman keep of Rochester's castle looms large and dominates the surrounding area. This is not surprising, for it is the tallest keep in England and its sheer size makes it the most impressive of all those visited. A wonderful view of the extent of the castle walls surrounding the keep is obtained from the approach across the medieval bridge over the Medway. It is well worth stopping awhile to marvel at a structure that is more than 875 years old and has survived three sieges and all attempts at wilful destruction. An earlier castle was raised on the site at the time of the Norman Conquest and rebuilt between 1087 and 1089 by Gundulf, Bishop of Rochester, for William Rufus. It was one of the earliest stone castles to be built and was protected on three sides by a formidable ditch, which can still be seen between the castle and the cathedral, and, fronting the Medway, by a curtain wall founded on the original Roman city wall. Odo, half-brother of William the Conqueror and

The arcade on the main floor of the

Bishop of Bayeux, led a rebellion against the king, which resulted in the first siege of the castle in 1088, with the Royalists victorious.

In 1127, King Henry I granted Rochester Castle to William de Corbeuil and the See of Canterbury in perpetuity, and a licence to build what chronicler Gervase of Canterbury described as a 'noble tower'.

The great keep not only served as a military stronghold, but also as the archbishop's palace and thus incorporated some of the finest residential accommodation anywhere. In 1215, Archbishop Stephen Langton refused an order by King John to hand it over, and after rebels seized the castle, John personally marched on it. The king attacked it with siege engines, but his stone projectiles achieved little in spite of breaching the curtain wall, forcing him to resort to undermining the keep, into which the defenders had retreated. But he needed fuel, and a command to his justiciar to 'send to us with all speed by day and night forty of the fattest pigs of the sort least good for eating to bring fire beneath the tower', had the desired effect and a whole section of the tower came down. But only starvation brought about a capitulation. The castle was repaired, but damaged again during the Barons' War siege in 1264, and although subsequently restored and improved by Edward III and Richard II, it had fallen into decay by the fourteenth century.

The keep is undoubtedly the most outstanding feature of Rochester Castle. Measuring some 21.3m (70ft) square at ground level, excluding the splayed out base, the rectangular walls rise 34.4m (113 ft) to the top of the parapet, with the four flanking towers stretching up another 3.7m (12ft). A round tower replaced the rectangular one destroyed by mining in

The view from the south-east, with the remains of the ditch

The west curtain wall

the 1215 siege. Built mainly of Kentish rag, with ashlar dressings and quoins from Normandy, the walls are a minimum 3m (10ft) thick, accommodating many chambers. A cross-wall divides the keep from top to bottom. A defensive four-floor forebuilding guards the first floor entrance to the keep on the north side. The keep itself had a basement for storage and three self-contained residential suites. The first floor probably served as the accommodation for the constable of the castle, while the second floor contained the principal apartments, with more elaborate decorations. A mural gallery surrounds this floor on all sides. The third floor was similar but less ornate. An almost continuous wall-walk is reached via a spiral staircase.

But, while the keep is the main attraction, there is much more to see within the castle. The whole stretch of the curtain wall on the river side is Gundulf's work of 1087–9, distinguishable by the use of uncut stone, frequently laid in herringbone pattern, with extra large stones forming internal buttresses. There are traces of a large hall and several window openings. The east curtain wall is pierced by two rectangular mural towers, and at its south-eastern end finishes in a large drum tower, all dating from 1367-70 in the reign of Edward III.

By Rochester Bridge close to Rochester town centre (OS reference TQ 742686). Tel: 01634 402276

Points of interest
1. Main western gateway through the rebuilt bastion
2. Gundulf's curtain wall on the river side built on Roman city wall
3. Great keep with the four-storey forebuilding
4. Henry III's drum tower
5. Eastern curtain wall with the rectangular mural towers
6. Castle ditch and the site of the main gateway for the east

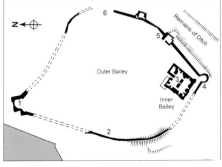

The square keep with the forebuilding

Scarborough Castle

The west view of the castle

From whichever direction one approaches, Scarborough Castle dominates the skyline. Standing atop a massive promontory of rock that rises steeply high above the North Sea, the scale of the ruined keep and the curtain wall stretching along the whole length of the headland facing the town is quite breathtaking. Being such a natural stronghold, it is not surprising to learn that the great headland has been intermittently inhabited and fortified since as far back as the Iron Age and long before the Romans, who established a signal station on the seaward edge. Exploration of the Roman remains can be combined with a castle visit. The Vikings later settled in and around Scarborough, and in 1066, a few months before the Norman Conquest, Norwegian king Harald Hardrada took control of the headland in an ultimately futile attempt to seize the English throne. The first stone castle was built by William le Gros, Count of Aumâle, immediately after he had been created Earl of York by King Stephen in 1138, but his tenure was short-lived. In 1154, Henry II appropriated all royal castles, including Scarborough, which had actually been built on a royal manor.

In 1159, Henry II began to rebuild the castle, spending the then massive sum of £650 mainly on

The powder store in Mosdale Hall

the construction of the great keep, which took ten years to complete. Additionally, he partially enclosed the keep and domestic buildings with an inner bailey wall; the enclosure was completed by King John with an outer wall. The so-called Pipe Rolls, the accounts of the royal exchequer, show that John made other extensive alterations, which cost £2,291 in total. He also built the long curtain wall and double ditches facing the harbour, and added a new hall in the inner bailey, a separate great hall in the outer bailey, and a chamber block. It became one of the greatest fortresses in England and remained a royal possession until the reign of James I. It became somewhat dilapidated in spite of intermittent repairs, and in 1312, it was besieged by rebellious barons, when Edward II's much disliked favourite, Piers Gaveston, took refuge there. He soon surrendered but was beheaded by the Earl of Warwick, having been promised safe conduct. The last king to stay at the castle was Richard III in 1484.

Scarborough Castle became embroiled in the Pilgrimage of Grace rebellion in 1536 against the forced suppression of the monasteries, during which it was unsuccessfully blockaded by an army of locals. Another doomed plot against the monarchy was hatched in 1557 by Thomas Stafford who, enraged by the marriage of

Queen Mary to Philip of Spain, seized the castle and proclaimed himself Protector of the Realm. He was captured after six days and hanged and quartered at Tyburn for high treason. During the Civil War the castle changed sides, but the Parliamentarians finally took control in 1648.

Access to the castle is via a narrow causeway over the barbican bridge built by Henry III over the double ditch dividing the town from the castle, although the original drawbridge has been replaced with stone. This leads through a towered gatehouse into the inner ward. The most prominent surviving feature is the great keep which, even in its ruinous state – heavy bombardment during 1645 caused the collapse of the western wall – still commands the headland. It was once 27.4m (90ft) high and had walls 3.7m (12ft) thick, with turrets rising above the battlemented walls. Spiral stairs connected all three floors.

The curtain wall still retains some of its towers, but the large polygonal Cockhyll Tower at the southern extreme was largely destroyed by a collapse of the cliff. An eighteenth century sally port passes through the curtain wall. Only foundations remain of the King's Hall and kitchen, but the basement of King John's two-storey chamber block, built in 1210, survives to give an indication of what it may have looked like when first built. The chamber block is more popularly known as Mosdale Hall, having been converted into barracks following the Jacobite rebellion of 1745.

On headland E of Scarborough town centre (OS reference TA 050893). Tel: 01723 372451

Points of interest
1. Barbican and gatehouse
2. Barbican bridge and gate
3. Remains of the great keep and forebuilding
4. Eighteenth century master gunner's house
5. Foundations of the King's Hall
6. King John's chamber block with the gunpowder store in the west tower
7. Sally port and staircase leading to the south steel battery

The great keep

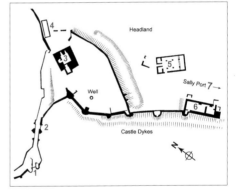

The barbican bridge

Sherborne Old Castle

There are two castles in the town of Sherborne, both of which have associations with Sir Walter Raleigh, but only the Old Castle is of medieval origin. Beware, most of the road signs guide you to the newer sixteenth century castle just 2km (1 mile) away. At the weekends, the Old Castle is a popular picnic spot for young and old, attracted by the many neatly trimmed grassy areas between the crumbling remains of the walls. The substantial site is surrounded by a moat and extensive earthwork defences, and much of the curtain wall survives to a good height. There is an interesting vaulted undercroft to the great tower, which is supported by a spectacular central column with a scalloped capital. The great tower had a staircase added in the thirteenth century, which was widened by Sir Walter Raleigh in 1592–4. The remains of the steps are now protected in an unusual way – by a covering of turf. The majority of the buildings forming the inner bailey have been reduced to foundation level, but the north range has been best preserved, with the remains of the chapel on the first floor notable for fragments of attractive interlinked blind arcading. The solid gatehouse, now the entrance to the ruins, impresses with its ashlar facing stone and arched entrance.

The ruins of the castle date from the early twelfth century, construction work having started in 1107 by Roger de Caen, Bishop of Salisbury, who, as Chancellor and subsequently as Justiciar to King Henry I, was a powerful man and the greatest landowner in the area. However, after the death of Henry, conflict erupted over the succession, and in 1135 Stephen seized the throne. Sherborne Castle was taken into royal ownership and remained so until the reign of Edward III, when Bishop Robert Wyville bought it back for the Church. In 1592, Queen Elizabeth I bought the castle from the Church and transferred the lease to Sir Walter Raleigh, who

had fallen in love with Sherborne. However, in spite of making some alterations, he found it uncomfortable and decided to build a new residence to the south. During the Civil War, Sherborne Castle suffered two sieges, in 1642 and 1645, on both occasions taking a heavy battering from the Parliamentarian artillery. After holding out for sixteen days, it finally surrendered to General Fairfax in summer 1645. Even though the damage was great, Cromwell ordered its further destruction, calling Sherborne 'a malicious and mischievous castle like its owner'.

On outskirts of Sherborne town, on minor road off B3145, Dorset. England (OS reference ST 647167). Tel: 01935 812730

The central supporting column in the great tower

The north range in the inner bailey

The fortified manor house

The great hall, with the original roof

More accurately described as a fortified manor house, more domestic than military in character, Stokesay warrants inclusion for its unusual appearance and its remarkable state of preservation, having been altered little since the thirteenth century. Situated on the English side of the strategic border area of the Welsh Marches, this pretty castle just begs to be visited and any driver is advised to turn off the road and stop awhile for what will be a rewarding experience. The castle takes its name from the wealthy de Say family, which owned estates at Stoke and nearby Clun and erected a manor house on the present site. John de Verdon, son-in-law of Walter de Lacy, inherited Stokesay in 1240 and is thought to have been responsible for the construction of the north tower and parts of the solar block, the only surviving elements from that era. In 1281, a rich wool merchant of Shrewsbury, Lawrence de Ludlow, acquired the manor house and began turning it into a splendid residence, taking advantage of the newly established peace on the border following Edward I's final subjugation of the Welsh in 1282.

De Ludlow tore down almost all of the original structure and replaced it with a great hall, a lofty 10.7m (35ft) high and 15.2m (50ft) long, distinguished by its magnificent interlinked timber ceiling, numerous large, glazed windows and an open hearth in the centre, as well as a comfortable solar. But he clearly did not trust the Welsh, nor for that matter any local upstart, for in 1290 he obtained a licence from the King to crenellate. The new defensive work put in hand was the construction of the sturdy, polygonal south tower by the west front, which rises 19.8m (65ft) to its battlements and has buttressed walls some 1.5m (5ft) thick. Access was provided by a bridge from the solar. De Ludlow also added a top storey of projecting woodwork to the five-sided north tower. The buildings were then enclosed by a moat, which was fed from a pond to the south-west but is now dried up, and a 10.4m (34ft) high curtain wall, of which only a short section remains standing alongside the south tower. A seventeenth century timber framed gatehouse now stands in the place of the original entrance. Stokesay Castle escaped destruction in the Civil War, its then owner wisely surrendering to the Parliamentarians in 1645, but later suffered from neglect.

Off A49, 3km (2 miles) S of Craven Arms village, 11km (7 miles) NW of Ludlow, Shropshire, England (OS reference SO 436917). Tel: 01584 875053

Tintagel Castle

Battered unceasingly by the Atlantic breakers crashing against defiant cliffs, this wild and windswept corner of the north Cornish coast remains an evocative place full of mysteries, many woven around the legends of King Arthur. The sparse and gaunt ruins of the medieval castle of the earls of Cornwall, perched precariously on its jagged rocks tumbling into the churning waters far below, overlie centuries of history where fact and fiction merge in delightful confusion. Romans certainly found their way to this bleak peninsula, and there may have been a Celtic fortress or religious community founded by St Juliot in the sixth century. King Arthur, if indeed he existed, could have been born at Tintagel after Merlin the enchanter had magicked Uther Pendragon into the castle to seduce the lovely Ygerna. The visitor is drawn to this lonely spot in the hope of fresh discoveries or just to feel the air of fabled romance that envelops this black slate headland. For these reasons alone, the half-hour walk along the uneven track seems like the beginning of an adventure into the unknown and should not be missed.

What is certain is that the fragmentary remains that straddle the mainland and a small island once connected by a narrow strip of rock date from 1145. First built by Reginald, Earl of Cornwall, illegitimate son of Henry I, it was virtually surrounded by steep cliffs and was spectacularly impregnable. Any enemies who made it to the narrow causeway, no more than three abreast, would have been faced with a hail of arrows from the battlements of the inner ward. Reginald built a great hall of which now only foundations exist, the hall having been pulled down by another earl, John, in 1330. The foundations also remain of a nearby chapel. In the mid-thirteenth century, Richard, Earl of Cornwall and younger brother of Henry III, erected two stone-walled enclosures on the mainland, with a main gate and curtain round part of the headland securing the inner ward. These are the most prominent remains standing today. The holes in the wall once supported fighting platforms for the garrison, but the ruins regrettably lack any form of architectural detail or ornamentation. Richard rarely stayed at the castle, nor did Edward, the Black Prince, when it came into his hands in the mid-fourteenth century. By then coastal erosion had already began the process of decay. When Leland passed by in 1538, he wrote: 'The residue of the buildings of this castle be sore weatherbeeten and in ruine, but it hath been a large thing.'

On headland 1km (½ mile) from Tintagel village, Cornwall, England (OS reference SC 048891). Tel: 01840 770328

The link between the mainland and the island buildings

The main castle on the island

Tutbury Castle

The motte from the north tower

The north tower

Situated high up on a flat table of rock surrounded by wooded slopes and a deep moat, Tutbury Castle overlooks a green fertile plain traversed by the winding River Dove. The castle's sparse remains, while providing a fine silhouette at sunset, would probably not make a case for a visit. However, its involvement in some of the most turbulent events in English history, including holding Mary, Queen of Scots, prisoner on three occasions, the first in 1569, more than make up for its lack of impressive masonry. To walk in the footsteps of some of England's greatest kings, as well as the lesser lights, provides enough encouragement to make tracks for Staffordshire. The castle, originally a wooden keep on a motte, was built soon after the Norman Conquest by Henry de Ferrers, who came to England with William the Conqueror. The de Ferrers succeeded to the earldom of Derby in 1138, and it was probably the 3rd earl, William, who replaced the wooden buildings with a stone keep. William supported the barons' revolt against Henry II, resulting in the castle being taken by the king in 1174. After another rebellion, Prince Edward, the future King Edward I, severely damaged the castle in 1263, which four years later came into the possession of Edmund, Earl of Lancaster. The additions, including the gatehouse, a great hall and great chamber, new towers and curtain walls were made in the fourteenth and early fifteenth century. Henry IV, John, Richard II and James I all visited Tutbury, which also harboured Charles I during the Civil War. It fell to the Parliamentarians after a short siege in 1646.

The entrance to the castle is by John of Gaunt's Gate, originally reached via a drawbridge. The red sandstone structure is now much ruined, with the top floor entirely gone, making it difficult to visualise how it may have looked when first built. Still impressive is the four-storey, rectangular north tower, even without two of its sides, which collapsed long ago. A stair leads from the vaulted cellar to a turret at the top, affording a magnificent view over the surrounding countryside. The south tower, known as Queen Mary's Tower, also survives to a good height and has some interesting windows and a large fireplace. In the centre of the castle grounds are the remains of the late twelfth century chapel, but nothing is left of Queen Mary's lodging and the receiver's lodging. Unfortunately, romantic though it may appear, the ruins atop the motte are nothing more than an 18th century folly.

NW end of Tutbury town off A50, 7km (4.5 miles) NW of Burton upon Trent, Staffordshire, England (OS reference SK 209291). Tel: 01283 812129

Warkworth Castle

One of the great Percy castles in the north, Warkworth stands on rising ground and overlooks the River Coquet, which loops around the village below its walls. By far the most spectacular feature is its great keep, the last major addition, built on an earlier earth motte in about 1388 under Henry Percy, the first Earl of Northumberland, who had been granted Warkworth by Edward III. Unlike any other in England, the keep is in the shape of a Greek cross, with a square core and projecting semi-octagonal flanking towers. Its defensive capabilities were clearly secondary to residential comfort, as can still be discerned from the lavish windows and complicated layout accommodating many fascinating rooms. The lack of natural light within the massive building was overcome by an ingenious light well raised in the centre. Still projecting way above the rest of the building, the open well also served to collect water in the basement for flushing out discharge from the latrines. The approach to the keep was by a passage under the uncompleted church and led to the porter's lodge. On the first floor, a lobby with stone seats, fireplace and mullioned windows gives access to the two-storey great hall from which a door leads to the chapel, which also extended over two floors. Steps lead up to the hall from the wine cellar, and a musicians' gallery looked down upon the assembled guests. The second floor, not accessible to the public, also comprised the solar and other private chambers.

Dividing the inner from the outer bailey was the unfinished collegiate church, now only recognisable by its foundations, flanked by more prominent remains of the West Postern and Grey Mare's Tail towers. Each has two deep embrasures through which longbows or crossbows could be fired, the five angled Grey Mare's Tail Tower faces the more vulnerable side of the castle. The adjacent stables may have something to do with the tower's unusual name. A gatehouse at the southern end protected by a drawbridge over the dry moat and a portcullis led to the large outer bailey. The gatehouse still stands to almost full height and has interesting pilaster-type projections on each side of the entrance gate. The Carrickfergus Tower in the south-west corner and the Montague Tower in the south-east corner provided both protection against attack and lavish guest accommodation. The remains of the hall are notable for the gateway tower into the complex and the Lion Tower, decorated with heraldic emblems of the Percy family, which was the impressive state entrance to the hall for visitors.

Located close to the Scottish border and for more than 300 years in the hands of the powerful and rebellious Percys, earls of Northumberland, Warkworth Castle has a history to match its magnificent design. It is believed that the first castle was erected around 1150 by Henry, Earl of Northumberland and son of David I, King of Scots. In 1157, Henry II recovered Northumberland from the Scots and gave it to Roger FitzRichard, whose descendants held it until the ascendancy of the Percys. After being captured in a Scottish invasion in 1173, the FitzRichards strengthened the castle, adding the gatehouse, Carrickfergus Tower, domestic buildings and the hall. The Scots besieged

82   *The great keep with the Light Tower*

The outer bailey with the collegiate church in the foregroud

it twice in 1327, leading Edward III to grant it to Henry Percy II in 1332. The Percys began to dominate Northumberland and made major additions to the castle, culminating in the construction of the ambitiously opulent keep. They also turned on the Crown and during a rebellion in 1405 Henry IV's forces battered the castle with seven volleys of cannon, forcing its quick surrender.

After that, the Percys became involved in several more transgressions, which resulted in the confiscation of their lands. But each time, Warkworth and other estates were returned to them. Minor additions to the fabric continued and the castle was kept in good repair it until suffered two sieges during the Civil War, the first by the Scots in the Marston Moor campaign in 1644, the second by the Parliamentarians in 1648, who slighted the castle. But the greatest damage was done in 1672, when it was cannibalised for building material.

The double fireplace in the kitchens

In Warkworth village on A1068, 10km (6 miles) SE of Alnwick, Northumberland, England (OS reference NU 248057). Tel: 01665 711423

Points of interest
1. Twelfth century gatehouse
2. Remains of the Carrickfergus Tower
3. Decorated Lion Tower serving as the state entrance to the hall in the outer bailey
4. West Postern Tower
5. Great keep, notable for its light well and myriad rooms
6. Grey Mare's Tail Tower
7. Montague Tower

The Lion Tower access to the hall

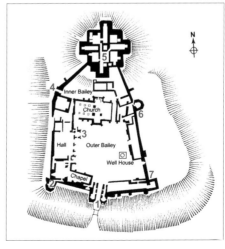

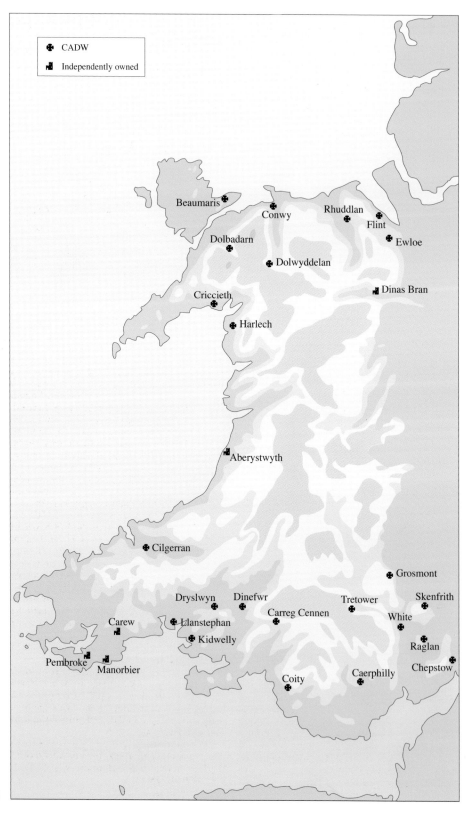

CADW

Independently owned

Beaumaris

Conwy

Rhuddlan

Flint

Ewloe

Dolbadarn

Dolwyddelan

Dinas Bran

Criccieth

Harlech

Aberystwyth

Cilgerran

Grosmont

Skenfrith

Dryslwyn   Dinefwr

Tretower

Carreg Cennen

White

Carew   Llanstephan

Kidwelly

Raglan

Pembroke

Manorbier

Coity

Caerphilly

Chepstow

84

Aberystwyth Castle

A general view of the ruins

There is now nothing left of Aberystwyth Castle but a single dilapidated tower in the inner ward, random fragments of the curtain wall and gatehouses, and a number of substructures which once formed the basement chambers on one corner of the fortress. The mint where Welsh silver was turned into coins for Charles I is said to have been located in one of these chambers. Yet, in spite of its jumble of barely recognisable masonry, its highly defendable coastal location overlooking Cardigan Bay and an eventful history should prove enough of an incentive to visit what was once one of the great castles of Wales. Its exposure to a constant pounding from the sea undoubtedly contributed to its poor state, as did several attacks by the Welsh, but it was the ruthless slighting by Oliver Cromwell in 1649 that proved its final death knell. During the Civil War, the garrison sided with King Charles I, and hence received no mercy from the Parliamentarians. Much of the stone was later pilfered for building works, adding insult to injury. With no permanent presence from the local council, graffiti is unfortunately beginning to spoil some of the remaining walls.

The Normans and the Welsh had built several early timber fortresses at Aberystwyth, but today's remains date from the reign of Edward I, who built throughout Wales to subdue the threat of Llywelyn

The fragmentary tower in the inner ward

ap Gruffydd, Prince of Wales. Laid out in a diamond shape, with formidable towers strategically placed at the corners, the building of the concentric castle was started in 1277 by the king's brother, Edmund Crouchback, Earl of Lancaster. But before it had been finished, it was briefly captured and razed in a Welsh attack in 1282. Incensed, Edward I sent his master mason, James of St George, to direct the rebuilding programme, and the castle was finally completed in 1289 at the enormous cost of £ 4,300. Five years later the Welsh attacked again, but were repelled that time, the defenders being sustained by reinforcements and supplies brought in by ship from Bristol. Already by 1343, when it was visited by the Black Prince, the castle had started to crumble and was no match for Owain Glyndwr, who seized it and other castles in 1404 in a last attempt to drive out the English. However, the Welsh held it for only a short time. It was retaken in 1408 by Henry V, who deployed cannon to bring an end to a siege begun the year before. But by then Aberystwyth Castle had lost its strategic value.

On promontory near sea-front in Aberystwyth, Dyfed, Wales (OS reference SN 579815). Tel: 0970 612125

Beaumaris Castle

This is truly a fairytale castle, its massive symmetrical towers reflected in the surrounding moat, with white swans serenely gliding through the water and views of the mountains of Snowdonia shimmering in the distance. Strategically located in flat marshland, Beaumaris, whose name is derived from the Norman *Beau Marais*, appropriately means 'fair marsh', and stands on the edge of the pretty town of the same name on the southern shore overlooking the Menai Strait. Before venturing into the castle, a walk around the moat provides spectacular views, but the full grandeur of the walls and towers can only be appreciated from the wall-walk between the fragmented battlements. The modern entrance leads over a delicate wooden bridge and through the gatehouse. The outer curtain wall and towers were built to partially hide from view the inner curtain, which is pierced by perfectly symmetrical towers and mighty twin-towered gatehouses guarding the fortress against attack from north and south. It would have been a daunting prospect for a foe to breach the outer ring, only to be confronted

The gate passage linking the inner and outer wards

with a second line of defence of such strength. However, this great feat of military engineering was never seriously tested.

Beaumaris Castle was the last and largest of the great castles built by Edward I in his drive to subjugate the rebellious Welsh, who had again risen in revolt under Madog ap Llywelyn. Designed as a concentric 'walls-within-walls' castle by the king's brilliant military architect Master James of St George, building started in 1295 and progressed speedily, but funds soon ran out and work was finally abandoned after thirty-five years before it was fully completed. It is fair to say that this unfinished masterpiece turned into a white elephant, costing almost £15,000 and employing at one time more than 3,500 people. With the marsh and the sea as the only natural protection, the castle was built with such strength and firepower that it was considered impregnable. The first line of defence was provided by the 5.5m (18ft) wide water-filled moat, with a small tidal dock created at the southern end. This permitted supply vessels of up to 40 tons to sail right up to the main gate. The old mooring rings can still be seen on the wall by Gunner's Walk, from which the dock could be protected. The 8.2m (27 ft) high octagonal curtain wall of the outer ward across the moat is punctuated by twelve round flanking towers and two gates, the exterior stonework from a nearby quarry at Penmon patterned beautifully in shades of dark grey to white.

The Gate Next the Sea still preserves some of its formidable defences, which, had they been put to the test, would have repelled any attacker. Confronted by gruesome murder holes, three portcullises and several sets of doors, the would-be-invader would still have had to run the gauntlet of a hail of arrows from above before reaching the inner ward. While none of the towers was ever completed to its planned height, the six

The moated castle from the north-west

The north gatehouse with the grand state apartments

massive towers and two inner gatehouses are quite awesome. Both gatehouses were designed to incorporate grand state apartments, but only those at the north gate were raised to hall level; the projected second floor was never started. Yet this is still impressive, the five great windows facing the courtyard giving an indication of an intended splendour that was reserved for the king and his entourage. The visitor is able to explore a large section of the passageways of the inner curtain wall, which is generally some 4.9m (16ft) thick and 13.1m (43ft) high. Another highlight is the Chapel Tower in the east curtain, housing a well-preserved little rib-vaulted chapel with elegant lancet windows. A remarkable point is that no well has yet been found.

In the Civil War in the seventeenth century, Beaumaris held out against the king, but eventually surrendered. A legend has grown up around Hywel of Llandona who, unable to accept submission and certain captivity, took to his horse and galloped over the precipice.

In Beaumaris village off A545 on east coast of Anglesey, Gwynedd, Wales (OS reference SH 607763). Tel: 01248 810361.
Web: www.beaumaris.com

Points of interest
1. Gate Next the Sea
2. Remains of the small dock with mooring rings by Gunner's Walk
3. Barbican controlling the outer ward
4. South gatehouse to inner ward with D-shaped towers
5. North gatehouse with state apartments lit by five great windows
6. Wall passages
7. Chapel Tower with the vaulted chapel

The narrow outer ward

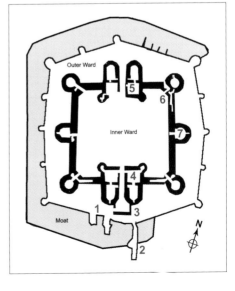

Caerphilly Castle

The main island with the formidable curtain and towers protecting the inner ward

This is a magnificent castle that, in scale and setting even in its ruinous state, has no equal in the British Isles. Spread over 12ha (30 acres), it is second only in size to Windsor Castle. One of the finest examples of combined land and water defences, and the earliest concentric castle to be built, Caerphilly ushered in a new, more scientific epoch in castle building. This precursor of the so-called Edwardian castles, surrounded by an artificial lake, introduced a double set of defences, with a rectangular curtain with symmetrical towers commanding an outer curtain wall. The imposing east gate, itself a powerful fortress, protected the inner court on the most vulnerable side, which housed the great hall and the private apartments of the lord. The island fortress was further guarded on the eastern approach by the outer main gate and strong dammed defences with fighting platforms. On the southern end, a great tower safeguarded the sluices of the Nant Gledyr brook, which fed the lake, and prevented enemies from drawing off water. The west gate led from the inner court to the western island, or Hornwork, which guarded the western approaches. The castle must have seemed impregnable, with the waters lapping the great towers. In spite of frequent attacks by the Welsh and slighting by Cromwell, it has survived remarkably intact and remains a striking fortress.

The inner east gate portcullis

The Norman marcher lord of Glamorgan Gilbert de Clare, the Red Earl of Gloucester, whose desertion of Simon de Montfort restored the Plantagenets to power, started building the castle in 1268. The aim was to protect the lowlands from attack by Llywelyn ap Gruffydd, Prince of Wales, who by then was overlord of all Welsh territories. But in the same year, Llywelyn destroyed the partly finished castle, and continued to threaten it during its fifty-year construction, until his death in 1282 led to a quieter period. Gilbert de Clare began to build again in 1272, but died in 1295 without seeing the castle completed. Caerphilly had to withstand several sieges during local uprisings in 1316, when Llywelyn Bren burned the outer ward in a surprise attack, and again in 1326–7, but each time the attackers failed to capture the island stronghold. The last siege, also unsuccessful, was by Owain Glyndwr in the early fifteenth century, who threw his last dice in a final effort to reunite the Welsh.

Henry VII handed lordship of the castle to the Welshman Jasper Tudor in 1485, and then to William Herbert, Earl of Pembroke, after which it gradually fell into decay. The fabric remained strong enough, however, to persuade Oliver Cromwell during the Civil War to drain the lake and blow up the massive towers. He failed on both counts, although one corner tower of the inner ward leans dangerously outwards, its inner side having been blown away. More than 700 years later, however, it still refuses to fall, testifying to the skill and quality of construction. Although in private hands throughout, the castle enjoyed much royal patronage and Edward I is believed to have visited several times. In 1326, Edward II sought refuge there from his Queen Isabella and her lover Roger Mortimer.

When the setting sun casts its shadows over the darkening walls, locals have often seen the spectre of a lady, with a sad story adding to the medieval romance. The ghost of the Green Lady has looked

The reconstructed fighting platform

out from the ramparts of Caerphilly for centuries, waiting for the return of her lover. She is said to be Alice of Angoulême, niece of Henry II and wife of Gilbert de Clare, whose neglect drove her into the arms of Gruffydd the Fair, a prince from nearby Brithdir who fell in love with the lonely French princess. Her secret, revealed in the confessional, was passed on by the monk to Gilbert, who promptly divorced her and sent her back to France, where she later died. Upon his return to Brithdir, a heartbroken Gruffydd the Fair is said to have waylaid the loose-tongued monk at Ystrach Mynach and hanged him.

In Caerphilly town centre, Mid-Glamorgan, Wales (OS reference ST 155870). Tel: 01222 883143

Points of interest
1. Main gateway reached via a bridge supported by an octagonal medieval pier
2. Water mill and south gateway and platform with vaulted gallery and well
3. Outer east gate
4. East gatehouse, used to defend the most vulnerable side of the castle
5. 'Leaning' tower, which withstood Cromwell's attemps to blow it up
6. Great hall and state apartments
7. West gatehouse
8. North-west tower with stairway leading to the wall-walk

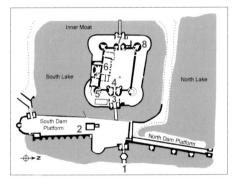

The west gate and the leaning tower

Carew Castle

Carew Castle is an attractive ruin, not least for the contrasting styles evident in its structure, which has undergone much reconstruction and additions during its memorable history. Unlike most other castles, which dominate the Welsh landscape from on high, Carew was raised on a small ridge on the flat lands around the tidal reaches of the Carew River, one of the innumerable creeks of Milford Haven. The principal reason for this relative accessibility was that it served primarily as the private residence of Gerald of Windsor, castellan of nearby Pembroke Castle, rather than as a baronial stronghold. It is said that Gerald, who acquired much land when Henry I divided the conquered lands of Pembrokeshire, obtained Carew Castle as part of his wife's dowry, when he married the Welsh Princess Nesta, daughter of Rhys ap Tewdwr, Prince of Deheubarth, in 1095. There is, therefore, some doubt as to who constructed the simple motte-and-bailey defence that first occupied the site. The marriage does not appear to have been a happy one, for the beautiful Nesta had many lovers, one of whom, Owen ap Cadogan, was slain by Gerald at a chance meeting.

After Gerald's death in 1116, the castle continued in the family through his descendants, the

Coats of arms over entrance

Fitzgeralds, who later called themselves Carew. But there are no subsequent records of the castle until 1212, when King John was said to have seized it for a short time when passing through Pembrokeshire on his Irish expedition. Nothing now remains of the original Norman castle, and the oldest surviving parts have been dated to the thirteenth century, when the castle was replaced by a square stone structure with a single courtyard, strengthened by four drum towers at the corners. The main eastern approach was protected by a barbican, which blocked the way to the gatehouse. The building has been attributed to Sir Nicholas Carew, who died in 1311.

Little of note happened until it was thoroughly reconstructed by Sir Rhys ap Thomas, who was given Carew and Dinefwr castles by a grateful Henry VII for his support when he landed at Milford Haven. Sir Rhys, then the wealthiest man in Wales, spent vast sums of money on building lavish new living quarters, including a very large banqueting hall. Over the entrance door are the arms of Henry VII, of Arthur, Prince of Wales, and of his wife Catherine of Aragon, later to marry Henry VIII. The reconstruction was completed in time for the last great Welsh tournament of knights, staged by Sir Rhys at Carew in 1507. According to chroniclers of

The castle from the dammed lake

The Gatehouse and Elizabethan north wing

the time, the tournament, spread over five days, was a splendid affair, being attended by more than 600 knights and retainers.

Carew Castle fell to the Crown when Sir Rhys' grandson was executed for treason during the reign of Henry VIII, and was later given by Elizabeth I to Sir John Perrott, said to be the illegitimate son of Henry VIII, in 1558. Sir John removed the top two storeys of the entire north wing and built five great chambers and a 40m (130ft) long gallery on the upper level, with a typically Elizabethan façade, notable for two rows of mullioned and transomed windows, and two large oriel windows. The stained glass must have been a magnificent sight, but the castle was now vulnerable to attack, although it held up well against the Parliamentarians before being slighted in 1644. It soon reverted to the Crown but was abandoned in about 1686.

Today, it presents two faces to the visitor from outside. The massive ivy-clad towers with their splayed bases remind one of its defensive qualities, while the Elizabethan north wing provides a contrasting view of extravagance. Inside, the early first-floor hall built over a vaulted basement and fine polygonal projecting chapel tower stand intact. The chapel on the upper level still retains its cross-ribbed vaulted ceiling.

On A4075, 7km (4.5 miles) E of Pembroke (OS reference SN 045037). Tel: 01646 651782. Email: enquiries@carewcastle.pembrokeshirecoast.org.uk. Web: http://carewcastle.pembrokeshirecoast.org.uk

Points of interest
1. Outer gatehouse
2. Inner gatehouse
3. Lesser hall and undercroft
4. Chapel Tower
5. Elizabethan great hall
6. North-west tower
7. South-west tower

The mullioned window

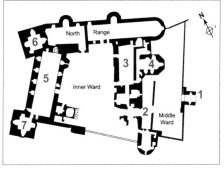

Carreg Cennen Castle

A general view of the castle

There is scarcely a more striking landscape in Wales – and there are many – than that spread below the sharp escarpment dominating the lush Towy Valley. Carreg Cennen Castle, perched high on the edge of the Afon Cennen gorge, which plunges 90m (300ft) down to the green fields, draws the visitor with an inexplicable magnetism. Although the climb is long and hard, and the heart pounds from the exertion, there is no turning back once embarked on the adventure. The reward for persistence, apart from having reached this daunting fortress, is the spectacular view of the Black Mountains. Not that the view was foremost in the minds of the occupants all those hundreds of years ago, for they were more concerned with ensuring that the enemy would find it extremely difficult to storm the castle. There was no way up the steep rock face, and the more vulnerable side was protected by an enclosed outer ward, designed to trap any intruders and prevent access to the interior. The huge north-west tower, the only round tower at Carreg Cennen, looms large over the ward and was undoubtedly used to reinforce this first line of defence. A hail of arrows would have rained down on the confined invaders.

But however dark and forbidding the castle may have appeared to any would-be assailant, it was breached and changed hands on several occasions during an eventful history. The early years are

The passage to the limestone cave

confused by a mixture of fact and fantasy, and the story of a fortress first being built on this limestone crag in the Dark Ages by one of King Arthur's knights, Sir Urien Rheged, Lord of Iskennen, is one of the many Arthurian legends. It is more likely that the first castle on the site was raised by the Welsh Lord Rhys, Prince of Deheubarth, in the late twelfth century and passed to his son Rhys Fachan, who lost it to the English when he was betrayed by his mother. He regained control of the castle in 1248, which was then seized in 1277 by Edward I, only to be captured in 1287 by the brothers Gruffydd and Llywelyn ap Maredudd. The castle appears to have been demolished soon after to make way for the imposing structure which is now slowly crumbling on the hillside, becoming Crown property upon the accession of Henry IV in 1399. But this too was severely damaged after being captured in 1416 in the Welsh struggle for independence.

Sir Gruffydd ap Nicholas unfortunately declared for Lancaster in the Wars of the Roses, and it was destroyed by order of the king in 1462.

Five hundred men worked to devastate it, but enough is left standing to paint a relatively accurate picture of the once formidable castle. The inner enclosure was guarded by the three-storey gatehouse with its twin semi-octagonal towers on the north wall, and the cylindrical north-west tower, both of which stand almost complete. The gate passage was

The south curtain wall perching on the sheer rockface

defended by a portcullis at each end, and there were several arrowslits between the heavy wooden gate and the portcullises. It was the last refuge during an onslaught. A first-floor-level walk connected the gatehouse with the north-west and north-east towers through mural galleries, while a wall-walk on the second level encircled the whole enclosure. Along the east wall are the remains of the hall, a kitchen with a large fireplace, the lord's private apartments and other domestic buildings. Beyond the hall is a small tower, which held a chapel on the upper floor. A long walled passage with deep pits crossed by moveable bridges prevented easy access to the prison tower.

The most intriguing feature of the castle to be discovered lies at the south-east corner of the inner ward, where a set of steps leads from near the King's Chamber down into a natural fissure in the rock, and beyond into a damp limestone cave. Much of the vaulted passage is lined with stone, but its purpose remains a mystery. Still undiscovered is a warrior who is said to sleep beneath the castle, awaiting a call to arms from the Welsh.

On minor road off A483, 5km (3 miles) SE of Llandeilo, Dyfed, Wales (OS reference SN 668191). Tel: 01588 822291

Points of interest
1. Middle Gate Tower and barbican
2. Twin-towered gatehouse with the remains of the two portcullises
3. North-east tower with fireplace and latrines
4. East range, containing the kitchen, hall and private chambers
5. King's chamber
6. Vaulted passage leading to the limestone cave
7. Round north-west tower
8. Remains of baking ovens and water cisterns

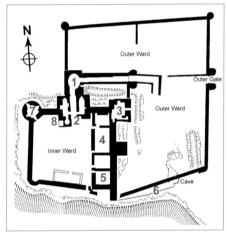

View towards domestic buildings and hall

Chepstow Castle

This imposing and immensely strong fortress hugs a spectacular sheer cliff plunging down to the River Wye, and can best be appreciated when approaching Chepstow from the English side of the river. The extensive ruins, stretching between the cliffs on one side and a deep and steep ravine on the other, provide clear evidence of various stages of development from its early Norman beginnings. The castle's size and setting also recall its great importance to the Norman thrust into South Wales. Only a few months after King Harold's defeat at Hastings, William the Conqueror conferred the earldom of Hereford on his loyal supporter William FitzOsbern, who in 1067 began building a tower keep on the central spur at Chepstow, then known as Striguil. The castle, probably the first stone castle to be built in England – although some believe that FitzOsbern's original tower was of timber construction – pushed the Norman influence beyond the old Anglo-Saxon border. William FitzOsbern was slain during a foreign campaign in 1071 and his son and successor, Roger, forfeited the castle to the king four years later, after an unsuccessful rebellion when he joined the Conspiracy of Earls.

The decorated doorway into the great tower

Chepstow was without an earl until Henry I gave the lordship of Striguil to Walter de Clare in about 1119, from whom it passed to his nephew Richard 'Strongbow', Earl of Pembroke and conqueror of Ireland, who held it until his death in 1176. It was in the time of the de Clares that the castle was massively fortified and extended with the addition of a bailey on each side of the keep. Further expansion, downhill towards the river and uphill beyond the small northern bailey, was initiated under William Marshall, who inherited Pembroke and became Lord of Striguil upon his marriage to Isabella de Clare in 1189. Among the most notable building work under him was the heavily defended gatehouse with its massive drum towers and a portcullis chamber between, which remains almost intact and provides an impressive entrance to the castle. Curtain walls extended from it and a round tower was later added at the exposed south-east angle of the ward. The upper end was also strengthened, with a forebuilding erected on the outside of a ditch which had been cut across the spur much earlier. This building, which was heavily fortified, could only be reached via a drawbridge and

The view across the River Wye

The hall block in the lower bailey

The sheer cliff face on the river side

effectively served as the castle's back door into open country. William also turned the keep into a great dining hall.

When the Marshall possessions were divided up among four sisters, Maud, the eldest, got Striguil and took it to her husband, the rebellious Hugh Bigod (the Bold), Earl of Norfolk, in 1245. But with the Bigods preoccupied with plotting against successive monarchs in East Anglia, Chepstow lost its importance and became merely an outpost. Nevertheless, between 1270 and 1300, Roger Bigod III built a splendid new range of domestic accommodation in the lower ward, which included a Great Hall and a large square tower with a richly decorated private chapel. Roger was also responsible for the town wall, parts of which still remain. When he died in 1306, ownership reverted to the Crown until 1403 when, under Thomas Mowbray, Duke of Norfolk, it was regarrisoned to meet the threat from Owain Glyndwr's war to reunite the Welsh, but was never attacked.

Only twice during the Civil War in 1645 and 1648, were Chepstow's defensive capabilities called into question, and each time, the castle failed to withstand the cannons deployed by Parliamentary forces, which battered the lower walls and the governors into submission. It had taken on renewed strategic value, serving as a vital communication and supply link between South Wales and the east for Charles I. Unlike most other castles in the land, Chepstow was not slighted but repaired, to serve as a barracks and prison until 1690. One of the most famous inmates was the regicide Henry Marten, who was imprisoned by Charles II in a tower which still bears his name. Because it was never slighted, the whole outline remains intact and several buildings still stand tall and strong, albeit without roofs and interiors.

Close to the town centre of Chepstow, Gwent, Wales (OS reference ST 533941). Tel: 01291 624065

Points of interest
1. Outer gatehouse
2. Marten's Tower
3. Lower Bailey
4. Great tower
5. Barbican and rear gate

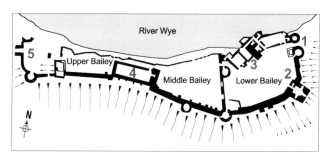

Cilgerran Castle

A general view of the castle

This, the northernmost castle in Pembrokeshire is built on a precipitous promontory, which dominates much of the lower Teifi Valley. Cilgerran was apparently built sometime around 1110–15 by Gerald of Windsor, Lord of Carew and husband of the spirited Nesta. It was then little more than a ditched and palisaded Norman enclosure castle, which served its purpose for a while but could not avoid being destroyed in 1165 by the Lord Rhys ap Gruffydd, the last prince to rule all of Deheubarth. The Welsh held the castle until 1204, when it was retaken by William, Earl of Pembroke, only to be captured again in 1215 during a one day assault by Llywelyn the Great, during his campaign to drive out the English. William II, the second Earl Marshal, won it back in 1223, and it was he who most probably built the present imposing structure, although some elements are of a slightly later date when the castle had passed through marriage to the de Cantelupes. By all accounts, the castle was derelict by the 1320s, but must have been refortified by Edward III, fearing an invasion from France, in 1377. It later came to the Hastings family, but reverted to the Crown in 1389. There is evidence that it was much damaged in 1405 during Owain Glyndwr's drive for Welsh independence.

Enough has survived from its battle-scarred history to make a compelling case for a visit, particularly when taken with its picturesque setting. On two sides, the fortress sits on the edge of the cliff above the Teifi, with only a nondescript curtain wall for extra protection. On the landward sides, it had two lines of fortifications. The headland was cut off by a bank and ditch which covered an inner ward,

A glimpse through the gateway

and beyond by a bailey reaching from cliff to cliff. The second line of defence is notable for two huge cylindrical towers, which bulge out from the high curtain wall. It is interesting to note that the outer walls are much thicker than the inner. Only the foundations remain of the gatehouse, but the portcullis grooves and drawbar holes for the gate can still be seen. A drawbridge crossed the deep ditch in front of the gatehouse. A passage in the curtain wall, defended with arrowslits, connected the gatehouse with the two round towers, and there was a battlemented wall-walk on top for additional defensive purposes. Two sally ports gave access to the ground east of the castle, allowing defenders to slip around the rear of the attacking forces. Little is left of the domestic buildings within the walls.

In Cilgerran on minor road off A478, 4km (2.5 miles) SE of Cardigan, Dyfed, Wales (OS reference SN 195431). Tel: 01239 615007

Coity Castle

Unlike most Norman castles, Coity does not dominate from the top of a high knoll, but sits on only a slightly raised plateau, from which a fine view can, nevertheless, be had of the rolling country all around. There would have been a Welsh timber stronghold on the site prior to the erection of a Norman motte and bailey, but few traces are left of these early fortifications. The story of how it came into the hands of a Norman knight (which may or may not be true) is an interesting one and worth retelling. Soon after the Norman Conquest, the South Wales marcher lord Robert FitzHamon, granted land to his favourite supporters, but one of his associates, Sir Pain de Turberville, sought out suitable land for himself. He took a liking to Coity and negotiated the acquisition of the castle and its estate with the Welsh leader Morgan Gam, who apparently agreed and offered Sir Pain two choices. Holding a sword in his left hand and his daughter Sybil in his right, Gam told Sir Pain that he had either to fight for the castle or obtain it by marriage. Sir Pain wisely chose the

latter and became Lord of Coity, probably towards the end of the eleventh century in the reign of Henry I. The castle's history was uneventful and in spite of its strong defences, served more as a residence than a fortress. The de Turbervilles remained loyal to successive monarchs and enjoyed unbroken ownership of the castle for 300 years.

During the tenure of Sir Gilbert de Turberville in the 1180s, Sir Pain's original timber castle was refortified with stone. This included a keep, a curtain wall enclosing an inner ward and the north-east tower. Few fragments of that building period survive, with most of today's ruins dating from thirteenth and fourteenth centuries, when extensive alterations were made. Although now greatly ruined, of note are the battlemented wall-walk connecting the three-storey rectangular keep, the fine middle gate to the inner ward, and an ornate annexe with fireplaces and latrines, which may have been the living quarters of the lord himself. Parts of the great hall and its service block have also survived, as has the east gate, an outer curtain wall and the round latrine tower.

The castle changed hands several times after the last de Turberville, Sir Richard, died in 1384, and saw its first real action when it was besieged by Owain Glyndwr in 1403. Leland in 1540 wrote that it was 'still maintained – some say that it once belonged to Pain, called for his ruffelings there le diable. Gamage is now lord, and it is his principal house.'

In Coity village, on minor road off A4061, 2.5km (1.5 miles) NE of Bridgend, Mid-Glamorgan, Wales (OS reference SS 923816). Unattended

A bank of cross-loops in the curtain wall

The castle from the road

The castle, with bridges over Conwy river

Conwy is one of the great Welsh castles, It stands on a solid rocky outcrop between the rivers Gyffin and Conwy and dominates the small walled town from which it takes its name. Although access by road takes the visitor through very narrow streets and alongside the castle, the best way to approach Conwy is on foot, across the suspension bridge designed and constructed by Thomas Telford in 1826. The eight massive drum towers, 9.1m (30ft) in diameter and over 21.3m (70ft) tall, are formidable, especially when viewed from below, and dwarf those who dare to come close to this impressive fortress. The misty mountains stretching away into the distance make a wonderful backdrop. Climbing to the top of the towers is one of the highlights of visiting Conwy Castle, for the panoramic view across the river estuary and out to sea is quite outstanding.

Round towers in the roadside curtain wall

While the walls and towers are all intact, they are not in a good state of repair, allthough they are safe enough to explore. The outer walls of the main castle are extended and enclose the majority of the town. Some 1.2km (¾ mile) long, with twenty-two towers and three original gateways, these are among the finest and most complete sets of town walls in Europe and, together with the castle, created a compact defensive unit.

Planned both as a residence and fortress by Edward I, Conwy Castle formed part of the king's master plan to control the rebellious Welsh through an iron ring of castles. Immediately after gaining control of the Conwy valley in spring 1283 during his second campaign, the king tasked his master builder, James of St George, later to be named Master of the King's Works in Wales, to design a combined stronghold of castle and town. Building proceeded at a frantic pace, with town and castle completed in just four years, employing up to 1,500 craftsmen and labourers at peak periods. The irregular and narrow oblong shape of the rock precluded the usual concentric design, forcing Master James to follow the contours of the eminence in a linear design dominated by eight virtually identical towers linked by solid walls up to 4.6m (15ft) thick. Additional protection was provided at each end by a strongly defended barbican, reached by a drawbridge, which was guarded by a portcullis. The interior was divided by a sizeable cross wall into two wards, each of which could be defended independently.

The heart of the castle was the inner ward, which contained the private apartments of the king and queen. Notable are the remains of the King's Hall, a beautiful little chapel to be found in the Chapel Tower, and remnants of further private rooms in the King's Tower. All royal living accommodation was grouped at first-floor level, but the floors are now alas missing. The most interesting feature in the outer ward is the 38m (125ft) long great hall, memorable for its sheer size and bowed design, necessitated by the narrow outgrowth of rock that dictated the shape of the foundations. A gloomy dungeon is found in the aptly named Prison Tower, and there are traces of the kitchens and stables.

Edward was in residence in 1295 when Madog ap Llywelyn became the latest of the Welsh princes to rise up against the English, but the castle, in spite of running low on food and the king and his men being trapped for several days when the river flooded, held firm. Edward and Queen Eleanor made several visits, the last in 1290 when, according to legend, the queen planted the first sweet peas to reach England. Once the Welsh were acquiescent, Conwy lost its strategic value and fell into decay. Edward, the Black Prince, carried out some repairs in the fourteenth century, Richard II visited the castle in 1399 after receiving a promise of safe conduct to meet his cousin Henry Bolingbroke, but was ambushed and taken to Flint Castle, where he was forced to abdicate. Owain Glyndwr held Conwy for

The Stockhouse Tower with the great hall

a short time in 1403, and during the Civil War, John Williams, Archbishop of York, was an ardent Royalist, was no match for General Mytton and his Parliamentarian forces, who stormed and took the castle in 1646.

By the river, E of Conwy town centre, Gwynedd, Wales (OS reference SH 783774). Tel: 01492 592358

The Prison Tower and Bakehouse Tower with the great hall arch

Points of interest
1. West barbican with the town wall extension
2. Great hall built in three sections and bowed to follow the line of the curtain wall
3. Prison Tower with the dungeon in the basement
4. Kitchen Tower
5. Chapel Tower with the little chapel
6. King's Tower
7. East barbican

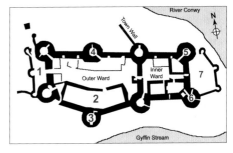

Criccieth Castle

Criccieth may be one of the smaller castles raised by Edward I to hold down the Welsh, but its commanding position on the highest point of a rocky promontory overlooking Tremadog Bay gave it a strategic value quite disproportionate to its size. From its lofty position above the small town from which it takes its name, it dominated much of the Lleyn Peninsula and provided a complement to the more substantial Harlech Castle, which on a good day can be spied across the bay. No enemy could approach unseen, and those Welsh hotheads brave or foolish enough to chance it up the steep hill would have been faced by the massive twin-towered gatehouse with a barred door that presented a virtually impenetrable barrier. And if that was not enough of a deterrent, a formidable tower close by the gate was topped by a terrifying and deadly siege engine, to which the attackers had no answer.

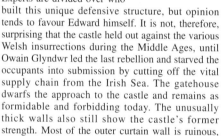

The gatehouse with its twin drum towers

Experts are divided over who built this unique defensive structure, but opinion tends to favour Edward himself. It is not, therefore, surprising that the castle held out against the various Welsh insurrections during the Middle Ages, until Owain Glyndwr led the last rebellion and starved the occupants into submission by cutting off the vital supply chain from the Irish Sea. The gatehouse dwarfs the approach to the castle and remains as formidable and forbidding today. The unusually thick walls also still show the castle's former strength. Most of the outer curtain wall is ruinous,

but the rectangular Montfort Tower at the south-east corner and the Leyburn Tower in the inner ward, still stand sentinel high above the bay.

The first mention of the castle was made in the *Welsh Chronicles* in 1239, but it is almost certain that the stone fortress was begun a few years before, probably around 1230, by Llywelyn ap Iorwerth, better known as Llywelyn the Great, who built the gatehouse and inner ward. The castle was enlarged with an outer curtain wall and strengthened by his grandson Llywelyn ap Gruffydd, also known as Llywelyn the Last, in the 1260s. But that rebellious Llywelyn lost the castle to Edward I, who, between 1283 and 1292, spent a large sum of money to build further fortifications, including the siege tower. Just two years after completion, Criccieth Castle withstood its first siege from Welsh rebels led by Madog ap Llywelyn, the Royal garrison being sustained with fresh supplies by ships from Ireland. But it was not so lucky when Owain Glyndwr attacked in 1404. After the surrender of the garrison, Owain tore down the walls and torched the castle. Evidence of this wanton destruction can still be found in the blackened walls.

In Criccieth town, off A497, 13km (8 miles) E of Pwllheli, Gwynedd, Wales (OS reference SH 500377). Tel: 01766 522227

The castle from the shore

Dinas Bran Castle

The castle ruins shrouded in mist

Towering majestically above the Dee Valley in North Wales, this rather fragmentary castle, reputed to be the highest in the land, is more imposing from a distance. But the steep climb, although not for the faint-hearted, is well worth the effort, especially for the breathtaking views over the verdant valleys far below – assuming there is a break in the perpetual cloud cover. The castle has probably changed little since Leland passed by in 1540 and remarked: 'the castle was never a big thing, but set, all for strength, in a place half inaccessible for enemies. It is now all in ruin.' And enemies there were aplenty during its short but turbulent history. There are conflicting records of who built Dinas Bran, but the prevalent opinion is that it was Gruffydd Maelor I, who started to raise a stone castle in the 1260s on a site that had probably been occupied since prehistoric times. From its lofty heights, the princes of Powys Fadoc ruled this northern part of Wales, much to the chagrin of Edward I, who sent the Earl of Lincoln, Henry de Lacy, to besiege the castle. The Welsh lords were forced to submit, after which the castle was set on fire and largely destroyed. After another insurrection in 1282 by Dafydd ap Gruffydd, the castle was again captured and given, together with the lands north of the Dee to the marcher lord John de Warenne, Earl of Surrey.

The gaunt remains of the castle high above the Dee valley

This was the end of the independence of the principalities of northern Powys, and the castle was never repaired. But in 1402, Owain Glyndwr unsuccessfully attempted to capture the site, in a last effort to reunite the Welsh.

There is little to excite in the fragments of the stone curtain wall that follows the contours of the hill, but the remains of the shell keep still dominate the landscape. An apsidal tower projects from the southern wall, which would have protected the most vulnerable approach, and two drum towers commanded the eastern entry. Scant traces can be found of a hall on the southern side, and of a barbican beyond the ditch, which guarded the entrance gate. But the allure of Dinas Bran, apart from its stunning location, lies in the many legends that have grown up around it. Tales of King Bran, the evil mace-wielding giant Gogmagog, and a golden ox and other treasures buried beneath the hill, add a veil of mystery and romance. Perhaps the final word should go to William Wordsworth, who described the castle thus: 'Relics of kings, wreck of forgotten wars. To the Winds abandoned and the prying stars.'

On minor road off A542, N of Llangollen, Clwyd, Wales (OS reference SJ 223430). Unattended

Dinefwr Castle

The castle from the site of the old town

A steep path winds its way from the town of Llandeilo up to the remains of Dinefwr Castle, spectacularly sited on the very top of a bold bluff, quite precipitous on two sides, with a still steep approach on the other. Alternatively, a gentler route can be followed through the parklands of the Dynevor Estate. Upon reaching the castle ruins, the track passes over a deep rock-cut ditch, which served as the outer line of defence and led to a bridge and outer gate, of which virtually nothing remains. Beyond the gate lies the outer ward, enclosed by a curtain wall, now almost gone. This is notable for two distinct level areas at different elevations that may have encompassed an early residential settlement and service buildings such as brewhouses, stables and barns. On the south-western edge, the ground falls away sharply, offering an extensive view down the flat land of the Towy Valley. At the far end of the outer ward, another ditch and the middle gate provided the inner line of defence, with the final approach to the heart of the castle guarded by elaborate flanking defences, which project out from each side of the gatehouse. A restored wall-walk affords a magnificent view of the surrounding country and Dryslwyn Castle, only some 6.5km (4 miles) upstream.

The inner ward comprises a polygonal area surrounded by a battlemented curtain wall that follows the natural contours. Within are the substantial ruins of two towers, the formidable round tower keep overlooking the cliff and river, and the equally strong cylindrical north-west tower in the corner of the encircling wall, both incorporating numerous chambers. The sheer drop made a tower at the south-eastern corner unnecessary, but a small turret was built later to overlook the entrance passage. The tower keep stands on a rocky outcrop, which forms the floor of the basement. Only the basement and first floor of the original structure from around the 1230s have survived, any upper storeys having been taken down and replaced by the thinner 'summerhouse' perched on top. The massive battered walls at the base of the tower give way to a vertical wall rising above a stringcourse of imported Bath stone. Along the northern edge are the shells of the separate and massively strong chamber block with well-preserved pointed window arches, and the similarly constructed hall, suggesting that this block was a later addition, or was remodelled during the reign of Edward I.

The history of Dinefwr goes back to the late twelfth century. It was most probably built by Rhys ap Gruffydd, the Lord Rhys, then ruler of a united Deheubarth. According to medieval Welsh law books, Dinefwr served as the principal court of Deheubarth. It would appear that nothing has survived from the original castle, all present remains dating from the time after the Lord Rhys' death in

The approach through the middle gate

1197, when the lordship was fought over by his sons and led to the division of Deheubarth and further conflict. Only a few decades later, in a letter to Henry III, Prince Llywelyn the Great referred to Dinefwr as the 'once famous now ruined' castle, Rhys Gryg, 'the Hoarse', who had eventually taken control of his father's castle, having apparently dismantled it. In 1287, Rhys ap Maredudd, lord of nearby Dryslwyn Castle, captured Dinefwr while King Edward I was abroad fighting in Gascony. But, when Edmund of Cornwall surrounded it with a massive show of strength, the garrison and Rhys'wife, which had been installed at Dinefwr together with the lord's treasure, escaped at midnight and left the castle abandoned.

The next hundred years in royal hands are unrecorded, but Dinefwr reappeared in historical records during the uprising in 1403 of Owain Glyndwr, who took the castle in a surprise attack, during which it may have sustained serious damage. There is no indication of its fate immediately afterwards, but by 1405 it was back in the possession of the Crown. A sum of money was spent on repairs and constables took over the running of the castle. Dinefwr was gifted in 1485 by Henry VII to Rhys ap Thomas, his Welsh ally in the Bosworth campaign. When Leland passed by in 1540, he noted it as 'now ruinous.'

1.5km (1 mile) W of Llandeilo, Dyfed, Wales (OS reference SN 195431).

Points of interest
1. Middle gate with a gate passage to the inner gate
2. Access stairs to tower keep
3. Round tower keep with later 'summerhouse'
4. Shells of the chamber block and hall
5. North-west tower

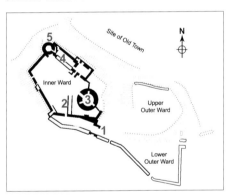

Sunset behind Dinefwr

Dolbadarn Castle

Set at the foot of Snowdon just past the popular Snowdon Mountain railway station, Dolbadarn would have controlled the entrance to the Llanberis Pass and the routes towards Caernarfon and the coast. It has a commanding position overlooking two placid lakes, Peris and Padarn. The only significant part of the castle remaining above ground is the cylindrical great keep, its dour slate exterior somewhat lightened by an attractively curved stairway. From the top of the tower, which can be reached via some slippery slate stairs, it is possible to see the plan of the castle laid out in the foundations of the walls. The keep now stands some 12.2m (40ft) high and has the same diameter, with walls 2.4m (8ft) thick. As was usual, access was via the first level, the entrance, heavily defended by a portcullis and sturdy drawbars across the door, probably being reached by a wooden ladder that could be retracted in the event of attack. A tiny trapdoor led to the basement. The upper storey may have had an encircling wooden walkway. There are scant remains of the curtain wall and linking towers, and the large hall with two open hearths at the northern end. To see Dolbadarn Castle at its best, take a short walk to the opposite site of the lake, towards the 'electric mountain' of Dinorwig Power Station, and admire the reflection of the castle in the still waters of Llyn Peris.

The round tower keep

Like Dolwyddelan, Dolbadarn Castle is closely linked to Llywelyn ap Iorwerth (Llywelyn the Great), who emerged as the ruler of Gwynedd in 1202. It was he who built the great tower around 1234 and spent much time at the castle. After his death in 1240, a fierce family struggle for succession ensued, and it was not until 1255 that his grandson, Llywelyn ap Gruffydd (Llywelyn the Last) gained the upper hand and was later confirmed as Prince of Wales by Henry III. However, Owain ap Gruffydd, who had lost out to his younger brother in the battle for control of North Wales, was imprisoned at the castle for twenty years. When Edward I succeeded Henry, Llywelyn refused to swear allegiance to the new king, who, in 1276 declared war. After Llywelyn was killed in a skirmish near Builth Wells in 1282, the castle was held by another brother, Dafydd ap Gruffydd, but was captured at the beginning of the following year by English troops led by the Earl of Pembroke. The castle was partly dismantled two years later and thereafter decayed rapidly.

On A4086, 1km (½ mile) SE of Llanberis, Gwynedd, Wales (OS reference SH 586598). Unattended

The castle rising above Llyn Peris

Dolwyddelan Castle

The great keep

The most challenging part of a visit to this thirteenth century castle is to find the path through the nearby farmyard that leads to the entrance, for the maps are quite indistinct. But, once found, the steep and wooded path soon opens out to give a clear view of the prominent rectangular keep that dominates the rocky ridge. Access to the raised doorway of the keep, once defended by a drawbridge, is now up a set of slippery slate steps, which require caution when wet. New flooring has been installed to permit a static display of Welsh castle history, and much of the interior dates from nineteenth century reconstruction work. Only the three first-floor windows are of medieval origin. A very steep and narrow stairway leads to the top, where the reason why this location was chosen becomes abundantly clear. It affords a commanding position over the Ledr valley below, which can be appreciated better still on a

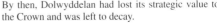

The castle on the ridge

short walk along the battlements. Originally two storeys high, the extra floor and battlements were added in the fifteenth century, when the castle was occupied by Maredudd ap Ieuan. The thick enclosure walls, which follow the irregular contours of the ridge and are protected by rock-cut ditches, and a second rectangular tower built against the wall, were added around the same time. A large doorway at

ground level and a fine first floor fireplace are all that remain of this tower.

The importance of the castle lies not in its buildings, but in the role it played in the early Welsh struggle against English supremacy. It was built by Iorwerth Trwydwn in 1170 to guard the ancient route from Merionnydd to the Vale of Conwy, but its most famous inhabitant was his son, Llywelyn ap Iorwerth, better known as Llywelyn the Great, who was born at the castle three years later. Llywelyn the Great joined the Barons' War against King John and obtained recognition for Welsh rights in the Magna Carta. By 1202, he had gained supremacy over other Welsh princes, controlling all of Gwynedd from Dolwyddelan. The castle was often frequented by his grandson, Llywelyn the Last, but fell to Edward I in 1283 after the prince's death. Edward repaired it and maintained a military presence until 1290. By then, Dolwyddelan had lost its strategic value to the Crown and was left to decay.

On A470, 1.5km (1 mile) W of Dolwyddelan village, 7km (4 miles) N of Blaenau Ffestiniog, Gwynedd, Wales (OS reference SH 721523). Tel: 01690 750366

Dryslwyn Castle

Few of this castle's extensive walls and buildings remain standing, but its location, high up on a rocky knoll above the valley of the Towy, makes for a picturesque setting. Sloping steeply on three sides, its fragmented walls are reflected in the river when approaching from a distance. Enough masonry breaks through the ground to enable the visitor to trace the outline of the castle, whose polygonal inner ward at the highest point was protected by surrounding lower wards, built under Rhys ap Maredudd, which hugged the ground sloping towards the river. The centrepiece was the Round Tower (Welsh Tower), whose walls at the flared base are more than 3m (10ft) thick. Unfortunately, the Round Tower has not survived to first-floor level. There was also a great hall, later replaced by a new hall, which was to become known as the King's Hall. New apartments were added, together with a projecting chapel tower at the eastern end. All these building projects turned Dryslwyn into one of the largest castles raised by native Welsh lords, rivalling any Norman castles of the Welsh Marches.

It was built in the early thirteenth Century and served as the centre of one of the three principalities that was once part of a united Deheubarth, commanded by Rhys ap Maredudd, who supported Edward I against the Welsh insurgents in the north. The first mention of the castle was made in the *Annales Cambrie* in 1246, telling of a siege by the senechal of Carmarthen, although giving no specific details. Rhys turned on the king in 1287, when Edward apparently reneged on a promise to make over Dinefwr Castle and its lands to Rhys in acknowledgement for his support. Rhys captured Dinefwr, Carreg Cennen and Llandovery in surprise attacks while the king was abroad fighting in Gascony, but paid for his insubordination when the Regent, Earl Edmund of Cornwall, mustered an enormous force of 11,000 men and laid siege to Dryslwyn, which Rhys had made his headquarters. The occupants held out for some three weeks, but in the end proved no match for the huge force ranged against them, bolstered by a great siege engine which battered and breached the castle walls. If Edmund, in spite of the comprehensive victory, was disappointed, it was because Rhys ap Maredudd was nowhere to be found. He was, however, captured in the nearby hills in 1292 and put to death at York. The castle was damaged in a Welsh attack in 1321, and although some repairs were carried out, subsequent neglect put it permanently beyond use.

8km (5 miles) W of Llandeilo, Dyfed, Wales (OS reference SN 554203). Unattended

The great hall in the inner ward

The view from the banks of the Towy River

Ewloe Castle

The Welsh Tower

A weathered arrowslit

Do not expect a massive fortification clinging precariously to a towering crag, for Ewloe Castle is hidden away in peaceful and secluded woodland, where the silence is only interrupted by birdsong and the rustle of leaves in the wind. Reached by a barely detectable footpath across a wild meadow, it is not surprising, therefore, that it still is one of the few undiscovered gems among Welsh castles. It is then perhaps also appropriate that the castle ruins have yet to reveal their true past, which remains shrouded in much mystery. Various theories have been advanced as to who built it and when, but the only documentary source comes from the *Chester Plea Rolls*, in a report to King Edward II in 1311. Payn Tibotot, justice of Chester, then recorded that by 1257, Llywelyn ap Gruffydd (Llywelyn the Last) had regained Ewloe from the English and had 'built a castle in the wood', and that this 'was in great part standing' at the time of the report. Other possibilities put forward imply that a motte-and-bailey castle was first erected by Owain Gwynedd, Prince of Wales, around 1150, which may have been converted to a stone castle by Llywelyn ap Iorwerth (Llywelyn the Great) in 1210. Moreover,

just as its beginnings lack solid evidence, so does its subsequent history and final fate.

Built on a sharply sloping side and surrounded by extensive earthworks, it comprises upper and lower wards, of which the upper, and presumably older, contains the main feature, the substantial remains of an apsidal two-storey tower, known as the Welsh Tower. The shape of the tower is typical of native Welsh castles, lending credence to those who believe that it was built by Llywelyn the Great. The tower had a forebuilding on its southern flank and was connected at the western end to an encircling stone curtain wall, which in part survives among the encroaching foliage. The polygonal curtain wall of the lower ward abuts that of the upper ward, and at its western point ends in a two-storey cylindrical tower set on a rocky outcrop. This outer work has been accredited to Llywelyn the Last from 1257, and may have replaced an earlier timber fortification.

1.5km (1 mile) NW of Ewloe village, off B5125, 3.km (2 miles) NW of Hawarden, Clwyd, Wales (OS reference SJ 288675). Unattended

Flint Castle

Edward I's first stronghold in Wales lies off the beaten track, but is a must for anyone interested in castle building and the ebb and flow of the struggles of the Welsh throughout medieval times against their oppressive Norman overlords. Overlooking the Dee estuary, low-lying Flint Castle now has a forlorn and forgotten look, seemingly sinking slowly into the sandy marshes that surround its broken walls. Yet, even in its present precarious state, it is easy to visualise what an impregnable barrier it must have seemed to potential attackers at a time when the waters of the estuary lapped its massive towers and immensely thick outer defences. Edward I clearly chose the site with great care, ensuring uninterrupted access by sea for reinforcements and supplies, and by land, where he also built a new bastide town to protect the weaker flank. The origin of the name Flint, or Le Flynt, as it was once known, remains a point of discussion, but could have been derived from the rocky geology of the area.

It was the insubordination and associated threat of Llywelyn ap Gruffydd (Llywelyn the Last), who refused to swear allegiance to the new king upon Edward's accession in 1272, that led to what was probably the greatest period of castle building in Britain. The king was in a hurry and employed some 2,300 well-paid workmen to start work in 1277. But in spite of his intent, the castle was not substantially completed until 1284, having faced a Welsh revolt by Llywelyn's brother Dafydd ap Gruffydd in 1282.

Another attempt to seize the castle was made in 1294, but to prevent capture by the Welsh, the constable deliberately burnt the fortress and its bastide town. After extensive repairs, ownership passed to Edward, Prince of Wales, in 1301, after which life at Flint proceeded in a much quieter fashion.

Two tragic kings are associated with the castle. In 1311, the homosexual and ineffectual Edward II received his favourite Piers Gaveston, and in 1399 a highly significant event took place, which will forever preserve the name Flint Castle in the annals of English history. It was here that Richard II, a courageous, cultured and artistic king, was forced to

The great keep

The north-east tower overlooking the Dee estuary

The castle approach from the town

The north-west tower

abdicate in favour of his cousin Henry Bolingbroke, who became Henry IV. Richard was taken to Pontefract Castle, where he died in prison, probably murdered.

During the English Civil War, Flint Castle was surrendered to the Parliamentarians, led by General Mytton, after a three-month siege in 1647 and slighted. This act of vandalism, subsequent neglect and the effects of wind and rain are responsible for the sad state of the castle today, but there is still much to see and admire. Constructed as a square enclosure, probably under the supervision of Edward's great master builder, Master James of St George, it had round angle towers at three corners, and a huge keep at the fourth. The northern and eastern flanks were protected by the waters of the Dee, while the landward faces were defended by an outer bailey and a ditch, allowing the Dee to completely surround the castle. The most impressive and probably unique feature is the Great Keep, which was separated from the castle by its own encircling wall and moat, accessible only from the inner bailey across a drawbridge. Unlike any other keep in Britain, it had a series of galleries around the central open core, which contained the chapel, kitchen and living quarters, with the top level most likely furnished for the constable and royal visitors.

Its walls at the base are a massive 7m (23ft) thick.

Access to the inner bailey is gained via the much ruined gatehouse which, although protected by double doors and a portcullis, was not the stronghold seen in the gatehouses of Edward's other great fortresses. The strongly defended keep was probably considered an adequate alternative. The three angle towers, all once three storeys high, are in various stages of disrepair, but all contain remnants of spiral staircases, windows and embrasures for arrowslits. Much of the battlemented curtain wall connecting the angle towers has fallen, although a wall-walk is still accessible from the north-east tower, which also contains the latrines that emptied out into the Dee.

Off A548 NE of Flint town centre, Clwyd, Wales (OS reference SJ 247733). Tel: 01352 733078

Points of interest
1. Remains of the gatehouse with a surviving archway and porter's lodge
2. Three-storeyed south-west tower with the remains of a spiral stair, windows and embrasures
3. North-west tower with smooth stone facing on the lower portion
4. North-east tower with two spiral stairs, one accessing the wall-walk
5. Donjon, or great keep, with the remains of galleried rooms surrounding the open core

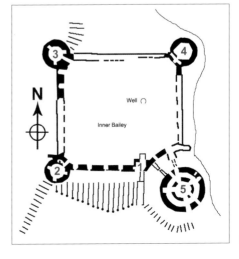

Grosmont Castle

The general view from the south-west

In contrast to low-lying Skenfrith, another of the trilateral Norman castles built to guard the routes between Herefordshire and Wales, Grosmont sits on a very steep hill that rises some 60m (200ft) above the Monnow valley. It occupies the western part of the high-lying plateau, with the remainder now taken up by the scattered buildings of the village, once separated from the castle by a drawbridge. The castle within the surrounding ditch is of polygonal shape and is accessed through the much ruined gatehouse, which does not appear to have been a strongly defended feature, being formed of two rounded projections from the walls connected by a recessed arch. The thick curtain walls and massive D-shaped towers have survived to almost full height, the most prominent being the five-storey keep, adjacent to the south-west tower. Instantly notable is the two-storey entrance, probably designed to confuse the enemy, since the entrance to the principal upper floors was at wall-walk level. Rather attractive is the isolated octagonal chimney, which ends in an elegant pierced lantern that allowed the escape of the smoke.

The octagonal chimney, with a pierced lantern

As with the other two trilateral castles, Grosmont's early history is somewhat indistinct, all present remains dating from a period after 1267. It may originally have been founded by William FitzOsbern during his invasion of South Wales in 1070, and most probably comprised a typical timber keep surrounded by palisades. After his son Roger was stripped of his lands in 1075, our knowledge of subsequent ownership remains confused until the castle and lands were acquired by powerful marcher baron Payn FitzJohn during the reign of Henry I. From Grosmont Castle, FitzJohn, is said to have ruled the Honour of Grosmont, which stretched from White Castle in the west to Orcop Castle in the east. The stone enclosure and great hall date from the early twelfth century, but the identity of the builder of both is still uncertain. The solid great hall has survived in remarkable condition, still standing two storeys high and retaining many features, including fragments of a fireplace flanked by two large windows, although any architectural features have long gone. This indicates that it was built as an administrative centre, where comfort was the overriding priority.

Payn FitzJohn was killed in 1137 fighting a Welsh insurrection, but before his death, he granted the Honour of Grosmont to King Stephen. The king lost it during the Angevin rebellion in 1139, when Grosmont was taken by Brian FitzCount, who three years later granted it to Walter, Earl of Hereford.

The ruined gatehouse and south-west tower

After the death of the earl, Henry II reclaimed the castle, which remained in royal ownership until it was given by King John in 1201, together with Skenfrith and White, to Hubert de Burgh as reward for his loyalty. Except for two periods when it was grabbed by William de Braose, Hubert de Burgh held the castle for thirty-one years, turning it into a formidable fortress by adding the gatehouse and three D-shaped towers during a two-year building programme starting in 1224. Henry III confiscated it in 1232, but de Burgh got his revenge the following year when he joined the rebel army of Earl Richard Marshall and Llewelyn the Great, which routed the king's soldiers camped outside the castle walls. Henry III, his wife and retinue were forced to flee in the darkness. As a result Hubert de Burgh regained Grosmont until his final fall from grace in 1239.

The castle passed in 1254 to Henry III's son, Prince Edward, later Edward I, who in 1267 transferred it to his younger brother, Edmund, Earl of Lancaster. Edmund was responsible for major conversion work, completed in a twenty-year period from 1274. The major elements were the demolition of one of the D-shaped towers to make room for an accommodation block and the rebuilding and extension of the south-west tower into a great keep. Edmund also built the famous chimney. After the death of his grandson in 1345, Grosmont passed to his heiress Blanche, who married John of Gaunt. In his final and ultimately unsuccessful throw for Welsh independence, Owain Glyndwr took Grosmont in 1405, but was defeated later that year by Henry of Monmouth, who became Henry V in 1413. Thereafter, the castle was left to decay. It is worth stopping by at Grosmont church to view the now much eroded effigy of a knight, thought to be Edmund, who built the church for his mother, Queen Eleanor.

In Grosmont village on B4347, 12km (7.5 miles) NE of Abergavenny, Gwent, Wales (OS reference SO 405244). Tel: 01981 240301

Points of interest
1. Gatehouse
2. South-west tower and keep with a double-storey entrance
3. West tower
4. Octagonal chimney with a pierced lantern
5. Great hall with the remains of fireplace

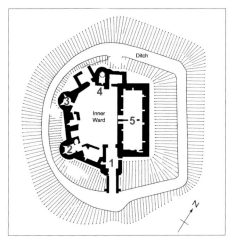

The keep, with its double-height entrance

Harlech Castle

Perched on a bold, rocky outcrop at the head of the Traeth Bach estuary, Harlech Castle is visible from miles away on the approach to the small town after which it is named. One can almost hear the stirring tune of Men of Harlech while trying to navigate the narrow, twisting lanes to the rickety wooden bridge over the moat, which leads to the massive twin towers of the gatehouse. This must be one of the most strongly built castles in the land, for the walls appear so thick as to be impregnable by anything less than a modern missile. The middle ward is narrow but affords splendid views, as the ruined outer walls permit a nearly unobstructed view over the sandy expanse towards the sea at Tremadog Bay. Once through to the heart of the castle, the experience is heightened by the neatly trimmed lawn of the courtyard, surrounded by a very impressive square enclosure, with colossal

The gatehouse from the inner ward

drum towers at the corners. Not to be missed is the wall-walk, which provides unforgettable panoramic vistas all around and an aerial view of the impressive inner ward and its buildings.

Harlech was one of Edward I's 'iron ring' of castles erected during his second building spree to hold down the newly conquered principality of North Wales. Designed by Master James of St

George, who personally supervised the construction, work started in 1283 and was completed in 1290. Set on the summit of the 60m (200ft) crag, it is a fine example of a concentric castle, with the lofty inner ward entirely contained within the much lower middle ward, which is never more than 9m (30ft) wide. Its four corners are marked by mighty 18.3m (60ft) high bastions, which rise 6m (20ft) above the solid curtain wall enclosure. The two western towers are topped by turrets. Built against the walls are the scant remains of two great halls, a granary, a kitchen and a chapel.

But the central defensive feature at Harlech is the monumental gatehouse, itself a castle within a castle. Rectangular in shape and measuring some 24.4m (80ft) by 16.5m (54ft), it comprises three storeys, and contained the main residential apartments. The many rooms can still be explored, but are surprisingly devoid of ornamentation. A narrow passage, flanked by semi-circular towers, was protected by two portcullises and seven sets of 'murder holes', and extends far into the inner ward, overlooked by the two circular corner towers which complete the gatehouse structure. The castle is surrounded on two sides by a deep dry moat, hewn out of the rock, while precipitous cliffs protected the

The approach to the twin-towered gatehouse

The site of the great hall

The wall-walk

seaward rear, where a path and fortified stairway led from a postern gate down to a dock. This permitted supplies to be brought by ship, in the event that access by land was blocked. Today, 1km (½ mile) of gorse-covered dunes separate the castle from the sea.

Harlech was besieged three times, but was never seriously damaged. The Welsh rebel Madog tried unsuccessfully to take it in 1294, but another thorn in the side of the English, Owain Glyndwr, had more luck in 1404. After blocking the land route while his French allies patrolled the sea below, he forced a surrender when, after a siege of many months, the garrison had been reduced by sickness and starvation. Owain then made Harlech his stronghold, facing a formidable English attack, which failed, however, to breach its defences. Starvation and hardship forced the rebels out in 1409. During the Wars of the Roses, the castle was held for the Lancastrians by Jasper Tudor, half-brother of Henry VI, and later by Daffydd ap Ieuan, but yielded to the Yorkists under William Lord Herbert in 1648, after the garrison suffered great hardship in the siege, which lasted several years. The song The Men of Harlech is said to commemorate their bravery.

In Harlech town centre, Gwynedd, Wales (OS reference SH 581312). Tel: 01766 780552

Points of interest
1. Remains of the bridge over the moat and the outer gate
2. Three-storeyed gatehouse
3. Garden or Mortimer Tower
4. Weathercock or Bronwen Tower
5. Path and fortified stairs leading to the water gate
6. Chapel or Armourer's Tower
7. Prison or Debtors' Tower

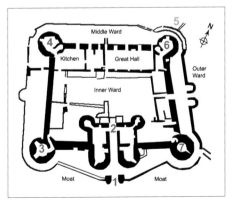

Kidwelly Castle

The view from the estuary

Long after this imposing castle was finally abandoned, its massive ruined walls and towers, three times captured and three times rebuilt, remain a powerful reminder of the mighty struggles between the Norman invaders and Welsh princes for supremacy over South Wales. Constructed on a steep, natural ridge at the mouth of the Gwaendraeth River, Kidwelly overlooks the flat marshes of the wide estuary and was one of a series of Norman strongholds positioned to command the main road to the west at river crossings. Before exploring the vast interior of the castle, the visitor is recommended to cross the river for an unparalleled view and to circumnavigate its walls from the outside, to fully appreciate the extent of the fortress that dominates the town and the green valley behind.

The coastal lands round about were granted by Henry I to Roger, Bishop of Salisbury, in 1106, and it was he who proceeded to build a typical motte-and-bailey fortification on this strategically important site. When he died, the castle appears to have been acquired

The oven near the north gatehouse

by William de Londres, who had assisted the bishop in the battle against Gwenllian, wife of Gruffydd ap Rhys, in 1136. The Welsh were defeated and Gwenllian and her sons killed. History then becomes somewhat vague, but it would appear that Kidwelly suffered a local conquest, for the *Welsh Chronicles* record that, in 1190 the Lord Rhys rebuilt the castle in stone. Over the next fifty years, it changed hands a number of times, being burnt by Gryg Rhys in

1215, captured again during a Welsh uprising in 1231, and passing to Patrick de Chaworth by marriage in 1242. The marriage of the Chaworth heiress Matilda to King Edward I's brother, Edmund, Earl of Lancaster, in 1291 brought the Kidwelly estate into the house of Lancaster, where it remained until the accession of Henry IV in 1399. The Welsh having been subdued, the Crown appeared to have little use for the castle. Henry VII granted it to Rhys ap Tewdwr, whose grandson forfeited it in 1531. It then passed to the earls of Cawdor.

It comprises two wards, the outer of which follows the contours of the mound. A deep ditch served as added protection for the semicircular curtain wall studded with towers on the landward side. A square inner ward with a strong curtain with four large round corner towers was created by Pain de Chaworth around 1275, but these had to be heightened later to provide covering to the new gatehouse, which was completed around 1402. The southern twin-towered gatehouse and main entrance to the castle is a formidable 18.3m (60ft) high three-storeyed structure which is now approached over a causeway from a small knoll. Its defensive features were impressive and included an inner and outer portcullis, murder holes, arrowloops, battlements and machicolations. Of note are the vaulted rooms and cellars on the ground floor, and the remains of the principal upper chambers. A smaller gatehouse, also of three storeys with two flanking towers, gave

The late hall and north-west tower

access to the outworks at the northern extremity of the castle, but this is now much ruined. Within the outer ward are several domestic buildings believed to have been erected by Rhys ap Tewdwr at the close of the fifteenth century. Two gable ends and a low wall have survived of a great hall, and there are the remains of a kitchen with two fireplaces and a bakehouse with a large oven built into the wall. The purpose of another large chamber erected in the angle between the northern gate and the east wall remains undetermined.

The inner ward is quite compact and is dominated by the tall corner towers. All eventually comprised five storeys and are in various stages of decay, the upper part of the north-west tower being particularly well preserved, with some of the battlements still intact, while the south-west tower retains its rare domed roof. A curious feature is a large chapel built out from the enceinte towards the river, its semi-octagonal eastern end supported by massive spurs into the rock. An unbroken range of trefoiled lancet windows are particularly notable, and other interesting attributes are a double piscina and wide sedilia on the south side of the altar, and a small sacristy projecting out from the main body of the chapel. There are the remains of a hall, solar and kitchen, which take up the whole of the eastern length of the wall. In the inner wall of the solar, the visitor can admire two trefoiled lancet windows and fireplace with quoins and a hood of dressed Sutton stone.

On A484 near Kidwelly town centre, Dyfed, Wales (OS reference SN 409070).
Tel: 01554 890104

The main entrance

Points of interest
1. Twin-towered gatehouse approached via a causeway
2. Late fifteenth century great hall in the outer ward
3. Bakehouse with oven
4. North gate
5. North-west tower with traces of the main battlements
6. North-east tower with access to the mantlet
7. Chapel built out towards the river

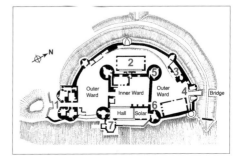

Llanstephan Castle

Built on the site of an Iron Age hill fort, this impressive marcher fortress sits on a high wooded bluff over the broad Towy estuary, within sight of Kidwelly Castle. The Normans were quick to recognise the defensive qualities of this ready-made stronghold, which is protected on three sides by natural sea escarpments and approachable only from the west. Even today, access to this rather well preserved castle is along a narrow rocky path that climbs forever upwards and seems never to reach its age-defying walls. It does, of course, and at its end presents the intrepid mountaineer with a magnificent Norman ruin that commands the sandy shores of the estuary and the lush green rolling hills behind. But more than that, it also offers tempting glimpses of the Iron Age earthworks hiding in the undergrowth outside its walls.

The castle is said to owe its origins to Gilbert de Clare, first Earl of Pembroke and Lord of Cardigan, who built a simple motte-and-bailey structure here in 1112. But its timber buildings and palisades proved no match for the Welsh raiders from the north, as its early history was marked by frequent attacks and destruction. After such an attack and burning in 1137, Llanstephan was rebuilt in some fashion, but was captured again in 1146, this time by Cadell, Maredudd and Rhys Gryg, the sons of the Prince of Deheubarth. The Welsh occupants surrendered in 1158 to Henry II. The king gave the castle to William de Camville, whose descendants retained ownership until the last de Camville died without male heir in 1338. The intervening years had also been full of strife. It was captured again by the

Welsh princes in 1189, and in spite of major refortification in stone from 1192 with the addition of two towers, a curtain wall between the upper and lower wards, and later a formidable inner gatehouse and keep, it fell twice more to the Welsh in 1215 and 1257. Each time it was regained and repaired. The present ruins date from the last repairs undertaken by Geoffrey de Camville after 1257.

After the death of the last de Camville, the third William, Llanstephan passed to Robert Penrees through marriage to William's daughter, Eleanor. By 1377, the Crown had regained control, but allowed the Penrees family to continue living there as custodians. Sir John Penrees strengthened the castle against a renewed Welsh threat, but had the misfortune to lose the castle to Owain Glyndwr, albeit for only a few months. After the death of the

The great gatehouse from the lower ward

The castle from across the Towy estuary

The inner gate into the upper ward

last Penrees in 1443, the castle again reverted to the Crown until Henry VII conferred it on his nephew Jasper Tudor, Earl of Bedford in 1495. Upon his death, it was allowed to decay.

Llanstephan Castle is a polygonal double enclosure, with the earliest upper ward taking up the smaller area at the steepest end and accessible only through the lower outer ward. The most noteworthy building is the rectangular inner gatehouse, which stands to its full three-storey height, with some of its parapet and crenellations still intact. The building is dark and menacing, being lit only by narrow arrowslits. The ground floor was heavily defended by a portcullis and double doors, and access to the first floor was via a wall-walk now largely ruinous. Only the foundations remain of the round tower keep, but the domestic buildings are better preserved. A large section of the surrounding curtain wall survives, although the eastern stretch that divided the upper and lower wards has fallen. The outer ward retains much of its strong wall enclosure pierced by two mural towers, one of which is now heavily ruined, a fighting platform in the east wall, and the impressive great gatehouse, built in 1280. The latter comprises two formidable drum towers linked by a three-storeyed building containing the hall on the first floor. The hall is notable for an elaborate fireplace supported by carved female heads, and for its fine windows, now unfortunately minus their tracery. The gatehouse was the *de facto* keep, fitted with two portcullises, heavy double doors, murder holes, arrowslits and guardrooms.

On minor road S of Llanstephan village, Dyfed, Wales (OS reference SN 352102). Unattended

Points of interest
1. Great twin-towered gatehouse with hall
2. Ruined west tower
3. Inner rectangular gate
4. Remains of round tower and great hall
5. East bastion fighting platform
6. Three-storey D-shaped north tower with latrine turrets and fireplaces

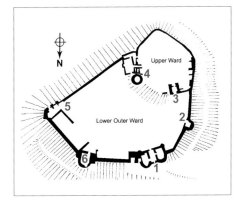

The lower ward

Manorbier Castle

The approach to the gatehouse

Giraldus Cambrensis, or Gerald of Wales, Archdeacon of Brecon, writing in his famous *Itinerary of Wales* in 1170, called Manorbier Castle 'the pleasantest spot in Wales'. Having been born there, his description may have been a little coloured, but ignoring the modern attempt to turn it into a holiday attraction with flower beds and roses climbing its walls, he may have had a point. The castle is set into a pleasant wooded area close to the sea and its battlemented walls and turreted towers still give it a romantic appearance. The name Manorbier is possibly derived from Mainaur Pir. Mainaur is itself a derivation of the Welsh *maenor*, indicating an extensive holding of land, while Pir seems to indicate ownership by Abbot Pir of Caldey Island, who lived in the sixth century and drowned in the abbey fishpond while under the influence of the local wine.

Odo de Barri, who accompanied William the Conqueror to England, was awarded the vast lordship of Manorbier and, probably in 1107, raised a simple earth and timber fortification on the site, of which nothing is now left. The extensive surviving castle ruins, a mix of baronial splendour and defensive stronghold, are the work of his son William, who acquired the lordship after his father's death in 1130, and his descendants. William greatly extended his influence in the area by marrying Angharad, daughter of Gerald of Windsor, steward of Pembroke Castle, and the famous Nesta, whose father, Rhys ap Tewdwr, was the ruling prince of South Wales until his death in 1093. Built on a slight rise in the shape of an irregular rectangle, Manorbier comprises an outer ward on shallow earthworks surrounded by a low enclosure wall, and an inner ward enclosed by a high curtain and fronted by a formidable gatehouse and two round towers. The gatehouse was protected by a drawbridge over the moat, which may have held water, strong battlements, a portcullis, arrowslits and machicolations, further boosted by an adjacent square tower and a barbican, of which large fragments survive.

A sixteenth century hearth and chimney

Many of the buildings, which are integral with the walls of the inner ward, stand to full height, with much of the battlement still intact. Unlike other Norman strongholds, Manorbier had no dedicated keep, suggesting that residential comfort was the major consideration. The central feature of the domestic buildings is the baronial hall, which dates from the 1140s and is notable for the massive carved fireplace and cylindrical chimney, and an oven in the rear wall. Private rooms open out from the hall on both the first- and second-floor levels. A barrel-vaulted cellar lies below. An ornate chapel with a crypt was built in 1260 across the angle to the south of the hall, and impresses with patches of medieval wall paintings, albeit now much faded, and the surviving piscina and sedilia. Both the hall and the chapel are reached via grand facing staircases, still accessible today. Nearby are the water gate, which allowed access from the bay whose waters once came up to the castle walls, and the latrine tower, which discharged into the bay. A Norman church, which offers the best view of the castle, stands on an adjacent knoll and the mill and fishponds outside the castle precinct are still traceable.

The view of the castle from the west

Only minor alterations were carried out after 1300 and the de Barris continued to live in peace at Manorbier until 1399, when Sir David, a supporter of Richard II, fell out with the new king Henry IV and had his castle and lands confiscated. After that, it changed hands several times among various court favourites, including in 1487 Margaret Beaufort, mother of Henry VII, until Queen Elizabeth I sold it to Thomas ap Owen of Trefloyne. One flurry of activity took place in 1403 when it was readied against a possible attack by Owain Glyndwr, but its defences were never called upon. During the Civil War it was captured in 1645 by Rowland Laugharne, the Parliamentarian commander, but by then it was already in decay.

Near Manorbier village centre on B4585, 9km (5.5 miles) SE of Pembroke, Dyfed, Wales (OS reference SS 064978).
Tel: 01834 871394

Points of interest
1. Old tower
2. Gatehouse
3. Guardhouse
4. Round tower
5. Ornate chapel with crypt below
6. Water gate giving access to the bay
7. Baronial hall and state apartments with barrel-vaulted basements
8. North tower

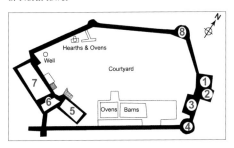

The castle courtyard

Pembroke Castle

This was one of the grandest castles in Wales, and even though it is now little more than an empty shell, albeit surrounded by an impressive array of walls and towers, few would take issue with such a description. The castle dominates a rocky pointed peninsula surrounded by the Pembroke River with steep cliffs defining two sides of the roughly triangular inner ward, the oldest part of the fortress. The third side, a substantial curtain wall with flanking towers, was once protected by a deep ditch, which was filled in when a large outer enclosure was added later, separating the castle from the walled town. For the most imposing view, the visitor should cross the river to see its walls and towers rising above the precipitous cliffs. The layout of the castle can best be appreciated from the top of the gatehouse towers.

The most prominent feature is the great cylindrical keep, which is the largest and finest such structure in Britain. A massive 16.2m (53ft) in diameter, its 4.6–4.9m (15–16ft) thick walls rise

The round tower keep

from a splayed plinth some 22.9m (75ft) up into the sky. A spiral stair within the thickness of the wall gave access to the five floors, none of which have survived, but the keep is still topped by its original domed stone roof, of a kind not found anywhere else, and two tiers of parapet and a central turret. In the north-east corner of the inner ward are the remains of the old hall and a more lavish and later great hall, which retains some fine window detail. A spiral stair from the ground-floor kitchens leads down into a natural cavern used as a cellar, known as Wogan's Cave. Also of interest are the western hall, which retains its vaulted roof, and the dungeon tower and connecting latrine block, but the gate into the inner ward is largely destroyed and the fronting ditch filled in. Surrounding the empty outer ward are a number of towers, some of which can still be accessed, and the impressive outer great gatehouse and barbican. The gate passage was defended by two pairs of doors, two portcullises and numerous arrowslits and murder holes.

Pembroke began as an oval timber and turf enclosure on the area now taken up by the inner ward, which was raised in 1093 by the Norman Earl Roger de Montgomery to enable him to control his newly conquered lands, which he left in the hands of his son Arnulf. The Welsh insurrection of 1097 found the lord absent, and it was left to his castellan, Gerald of Windsor, to defend the besieged castle, which he did successfully. However, the de Montgomerys were implicated in a later rebellion, giving cause for Henry I to confiscate all their possessions in 1102. The king then gave Pembroke to Gerald of Windsor, who became a wealthy man and may have been responsible for replacing the timber palisade with a stone enceinte. He kept control of the castle until King Stephen granted it to Gilbert de Clare in 1138, and with it created the earldom of Pembroke. The second earl, Richard 'Strongbow' de Clare, launched the Norman invasion of Ireland from Pembroke Castle in 1169.

Above: *The barbican approach to the great gatehouse*   Below: *The courthouse, great hall and latrine tower*

William Marshall became Earl of Pembroke by marrying Richard's daughter, Isabel, in 1199. The earl was a powerful figure and confidant of three kings of England – Henry II, Richard I (Lionheart) and John – and regent for Henry III. He and his sons continued adding to the castle's defences and domestic buildings, including the semicircular towers to the inner curtain. The extensive curtain wall, pierced by six towers, and a fine gatehouse that enclosed the outer ward was erected under William de Valence, half-brother of Henry III, who came to the earldom in 1269. Pembroke's history over the next almost four centuries was uneventful on the military front, but was notable for the birth of Henry Tudor, who became Henry VII in 1485. The present ruined state is due to severe slighting by Oliver Cromwell during the Civil War in 1648. Cromwell himself laid siege to the castle, which survived his bombardment but was surrendered after he cut off the water supply.

West end of Pembroke town, Dyfed, Wales (OS reference SM 982016). Tel: 01646 681510. Web: www.pembrokecastle.co.uk

Points of interest
1. Twin-towered great gatehouse with barbican
2. Henry VII Tower
3. Monkton Tower
4. Inner gate
5. Western hall with vaulted roof, fireplace and latrine
6. Circular keep retaining its unique stone dome roof
7. Remains of the great hall and stairs leading to Wogan's Cave
8. Dungeon tower and latrine block
9. St Anne's Bastion and postern gate

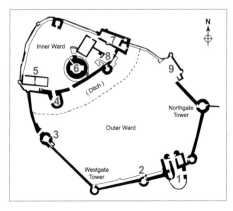

Raglan Castle

The south gate and Yellow Tower of Gwent

This splendid late medieval structure, with some justification regarded as one of the finest in Britain, was one of the last 'true' castles to be built. If its highly ornamental decorations still have a strongly typical French flourish, this is easily explained. Sir William ap Thomas, who gained fame fighting alongside Henry V at Agincourt, was deeply impressed by the local architecture and no doubt saw its construction as an appropriate expression of his new social standing. It is thought that prior to his intervention, a simple motte-and-bailey fortification had existed on the site, probably since 1070, but was then replaced by a defended manor house. But the romantic ruin now lording it over the surrounding countryside, is the palatial fortress built by ap Thomas and his son, Sir William Herbert, Earl of Pembroke, and continued by other family members. Designed as a military stronghold, with work starting in 1435, continual additions and remodelling turned Raglan into a grand Tudor palace. The wall-walks and moat-walks are an excellent way to appreciate the castle in all its battered glory.

Interestingly, the castle is still dominated by the ruins of the massive hexagonal keep, the first structure to be built and one which with subsequent additions was rendered virtually impregnable. Even 8kg (18lb) cannonballs made little impression on its

The arms of the 3rd Earl of Worcester

strong walls in a heavy bombardment during the Civil War.

The Yellow Tower of Gwent, so named after the pale sandstone from the Wye valley used in its construction, originally had three floors above the basement, with a fourth added later, and was equipped with a battlemented parapet around the top. The strong tapered walls, 3m (10ft) thick at the base and faced with ashlar, incorporated a spiral stair that led to the main room on each floor and to some smaller chambers. Only fragments remain of a close-in hexagonal curtain wall with six round turreted corner towers, with a height just below the arrowslit and gunport openings at ground level. The whole was set in a deep and broad moat still filled with water. Access was at first provided by a double drawbridge that crossed the moat, but this was replaced by a stone bridge when construction of the main body of the castle was begun in 1450.

The great Tudor castle comprises two vast courts arranged side by side, the richly machicolated red sandstone buildings providing a stunning backdrop to the yellow tower lying outside its walls. A great gatehouse consisting of two four-storey pentagonal towers, joined by a battlemented portcullis chamber above the gate passage, guarded the main entrance into the north-eastern Pitched Stone Court. The gatehouse is flanked by the three-storeyed Closet

Tower and by the attic that once held the castle's impressive library, and is notable for its large Tudor windows and rich heraldic carvings. Round gunports can be found in the lower part of the gatehouse and tower. Huge ovens and fireplaces have survived in the kitchens in the corner tower at the far end of the court. The Pitched Stone Court is separated from the Fountain Court by the sumptuous great hall complex, which has survived in a surprisingly good state, given the deliberate targeting by the Parliamentarian cannons. The great hall, 20.1m (66ft) long and 8.5m (28ft) wide, is impressive enough, but it is surpassed by the lord's private dining room on the upper level and the adjacent 38.4m (126ft) long Tudor Gallery with its magnificent traceried windows. Both retain many vestiges of stone carvings and sculpted detail. The Fountain Court, so named after a marble fountain that once stood at its centre, was accessed by the rectangular south gate, but could also be reached by a passage under the hall block.

Raglan was garrisoned for the king at the outbreak of the Civil War and Charles I stayed three times in the regal apartments on the western side of Fountain Court in 1645. Although the then owner, the Marquess of Worcester, spent lavishly in the support of the king's cause, Sir Thomas Fairfax forced a surrender after a long siege the following year. Cromwell's demolition gangs soon began their destructive work, but parts of the immensely strong Yellow Tower only fell after mining.

Points of interest
1. Yellow Tower of Gwent surrounded by a hexagonal curtain and a broad moat
2. Great gatehouse of polygonal towers with a portcullised passage
3. Three-storeyed Closet Tower
4. Attic library with fine Tudor windows
5. North tower with the remains of ovens and fireplace
6. Great hall, including the lord's dining room with carved decorations
7. Tudor Gallery, retaining traceried mullioned windows
8. Rectangular south gate

The rear of the great gatehouse range with the Closet Tower

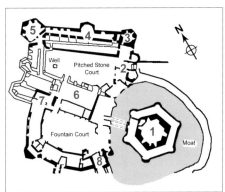

The moat-walk

Rhuddlan Castle

By far the best view of this castle is from the riverside, where the three large remaining drum towers are outlined boldly against the sky. Designed as a concentric castle, there is now little left of the polygonal outer defences protected by a moat, which was dry except for a short section to the south, probably used as a dock. The castle was able to obtain supplies by sea over 3km (2 miles) away, owing to a channel dug deep through the shallow meandering Clwyd, a project that took three years to complete. The much higher and thicker inner walls still stand largely to full height and constitute the majority of the remaining structure. Diamond-shaped, this inner ward had two double-towered gatehouses at opposing corners, with single round towers at the other two corners. The walls exhibit an interesting contrast between the warm red sandstone core and the grey stone covering. The main buildings of the castle were grouped against the inner walls, and included the great hall, private apartments, a kitchen and a chapel, but these can now only be traced through their foundations.

A wooden Norman motte-and-bailey castle rose in 1073 over the ruins of an older Welsh fort at this strategic crossing point of the river. This was the work of Robert of Rhuddlan, a nephew of Hugh d'Avaranches, Earl of Chester, and remnants can still be seen to the south of the present castle, which was begun by Edward I during his first Welsh campaign in 1277 after forcing the surrender of Llywelyn ap Gruffydd, Prince of Wales. Having made it his headquarters, the King and Queen Eleanor often resided at Rhuddlan. At the end of the fourteenth century, Richard II, was brought here on his way to meet Henry Bolingbroke at Flint.

After completing the castle in spring 1282, Edward faced another Welsh uprising, when Dafydd, Llywelyn's brother, attacked the castle but was beaten back. Within the year, Llywelyn had been killed near Builth Wells and Dafydd captured and executed at Shrewsbury, leading to a more peaceful period. Rhuddlan came under attack again in 1294, and once more in 1400 by Owain Glyndwr, but held out against the Welsh on both occasions. During the Civil War, the royal garrison was forced to capitulate to the Parliamentarians, led by the redoubtable Colonel Mytton, in 1646. Two years later, it was slighted by order of Parliament.

On minor road a short distance from Rhuddlan village centre, Clwyd, Wales (OS reference SJ 024779). Tel: 01745 590777

The courtyard chimney glimpsed through the sandstone wall

The castle from the riverside

Skenfrith Castle

The castle nestling in a wooded valley

This is the smallest of the trilateral Norman castles – the others are Grosmont and White – raised to secure Gwent against the unruly Welsh. Unlike the other two, where the builder took advantage of the presence of higher ground, Skenfrith was deliberately sited in a depression close to the Monnow river on the east side, providing an opportunity to harness the waters to form a 6m (20ft) deep paved moat around the enclosure. The little castle is a compact quadrangle with four drum towers at the corners and another solid half-round tower of a later date set into the west wall. Both walls and towers have survived remarkably well, standing mostly to wall-walk level and guarding the circular keep within. The two-storey keep stands 12.2m (40ft) tall, but was almost certainly higher when first built. Among its interesting and unusual features are the semicircular stairs built into one of the buttresses, and the fine, high batter that also marks three of the enclosure walls. Both are typical of the construction undertaken by Hugh de Burgh, who owned Skenfrith in the first years of the thirteenth century. Nothing is left of the buildings within the ward, but the hall from the earlier castle has been excavated, revealing amazingly well-preserved doors and windows. The remains of a large semicircular oven can also still be discerned in the north-east corner, probably part of the kitchen near the water gate.

The round keep

No record exists of the castle's foundation, but a motte-and-bailey fortification almost certainly existed in the time of Henry I. In 1187, Henry II tasked the engineer Ralph Grosmont to rebuild the castle in stone, but work was stopped the following year with only the east wall and the north-east tower finished. William de Braose completed the enclosure in 1193 by erecting a palisade around the other three sides. Hubert de Burgh was granted Skenfrith, along with Grosmont and White, by King John in 1201, and in 1219 completed the quadrangular enclosure in stone, also adding the four drum towers. However, within the year, heavy flooding in the Monnow valley devastated the castle and de Burgh filled the interior with river gravel and built a new one on top, including the keep. Skenfrith was given by Henry III to his son, Prince Edward, later Edward I in 1254, who added the solid tower in the west wall. When the final Welsh threat of Owain Glyndwr in 1403 had passed, the castle was abandoned.

On B4521 in Skenfrith village, 9.5km (6 miles) NW of Monmouth, Gwent, Wales (OS reference 457202). Tel: 01874 625515

Tretower Castle

This small ruined castle sits atop a low gravel knoll surrounded by rather damp meadows, and while it provides a pretty focal point in the shadows of the Black Mountains, it does not appear to have had any significant strategic value. This should not, however, deflect the visitor, who is rewarded not only with a romantic ruin, but also with a splendid manor house, Tretower Court, built alongside to ensure more comfortable living for the lord. The history of the castle, known as Stradewy until the early 1400s, dates back to around 1100 when Sir Miles de Picard, a Senlac knight, raised a typical motte-and-bailey fortification with a wooden keep to protect his estates in the Marches, which were acquired when he helped Bernard Neufmarché conquer Brecknock. Timber palisades surrounded the summit of the motte and crowned the bank of the roughly triangular bailey that lay to the east. The soft earth mound was revetted with rough stone to prevent it sliding into the 9m (30ft) wide ditch filled

A wooden bridge connected a door in the keep to the wall-walk

with water. Sir Miles' grandson, John, probably surrounded the summit with a thick stone shell and rectangular gate-tower in the mid-twelfth century, and also added a stone curtain wall with towers enclosing the bailey. An L-shaped hall and solar block, together with a kitchen, were built against the outer shell to the south-west, but a lofty cylindrical tower now stands in their place.

There is much speculation over the period leading up to the construction of the tower in about 1220–30. It has been suggested that the castle was sacked either by Rhys ap Gruffydd, The Lord Rhys, Prince of Deheubarth, just before his death in 1197, or by Llwelwyn ap Iorwerth (Llewelwyn the Great) in 1216. But the inner walls of the hall and solar may simply have been pulled down by Roger Picard to make space for the 21.3m (70ft) tall tower, which comprises three storeys and a basement, with walls 2.7m (9ft) thick on a splayed plinth. The fireplace on the first floor, with a sloping hood of ashlar stone supported on corbels, is particularly notable. A short, bridged connection was provided from the tower to the parapeted wall-walk, parts of which survive on the west side. The castle may have fallen into Welsh hands for a short while during an uprising in 1322, and came under attack again by Owain Glyndwr in 1404, although this was successfully rebuffed. Not long afterwards, it passed to Sir Roger Vaughan, who remodelled the manor house, built in the fourteenth century to serve as the lord's residence.

In Tretower village on A479, 16km (10 miles) SE of Brecon, Powys, Wales (OS reference SO 184212). Tel: 01874 730279

The great tower rising from within the outer shell

White Castle

The view of the moated castle

One of the three so-called trilateral Norman castles built to secure Gwent, White Castle sits atop a pronounced hill guarding a pass across the Skerrid Fawr mountains on the road from Abergavenny to Monmouth. The well-preserved stronghold dominates the beautiful, if remote, rural countryside surrounding its formidable towers and it is quite surprising that it is not one of the better-known Welsh castles. Its Welsh name of Castell Gwyn is said to be derived from a local prince, Gwyn ap Gwaethfoed, who ruled the land in Norman times, but it is better known as White, from its white plaster rendering, traces of which remain on parts of the curtain walls. The earthworks comprise three separate wards, the inner pear-shaped enclosure on the summit of the hill being flanked by a northern ward protected by its own encircling curtain wall, cylindrical towers and outer gateway, and by a crescent-shaped southern hornwork. All three are moated, with the inner and southern wards enclosed by a single revetted moat, which also separates the two. The main defences of the castle are those guarding the inner ward and comprise a strong curtain wall with four cylindrical flanking towers and a twin-towered gatehouse. The view from the top of the gatehouse is wonderful.

Before the completion around 1184–6 of the inner curtain walls and square great tower, of which only the foundations now remain, a simple timber fortification with a wooden tower may have been put up earlier that century by Pain FitzJohn in the time of Henry I. In 1201, King John granted the castle to Hubert de Burgh, who held it until 1232, when it was requisitioned by the Crown together with Skenfrith and Grosmont. In the later years of King John's unpopular reign, the castle was briefly captured by William de Braose. All three castles passed in 1254 to Henry III's son, Prince Edward,

The oven in the brewhouse

later Edward I, who in 1267 transferred them to his younger brother, Edmund, Earl of Lancaster. At that time, Llywelyn the Last mounted a major rebellion against the English and, being under threat, White Castle was strengthened with the insertion into the inner curtain wall of the towers and gatehouse. After Edward I finally subdued the Welsh prince in 1282, the castle lost its military significance, only coming into the spotlight again in 1403 during the failed uprising of Owain Glyndwr. When that danger had passed, White Castle was abandoned and left to the elements.

On minor road off B4233 at Llantilio Crossenny, 9.5km (6 miles) E of Abergavenny, Gwent, Wales (OS reference SI 380168). Tel: 01600 780380

Index